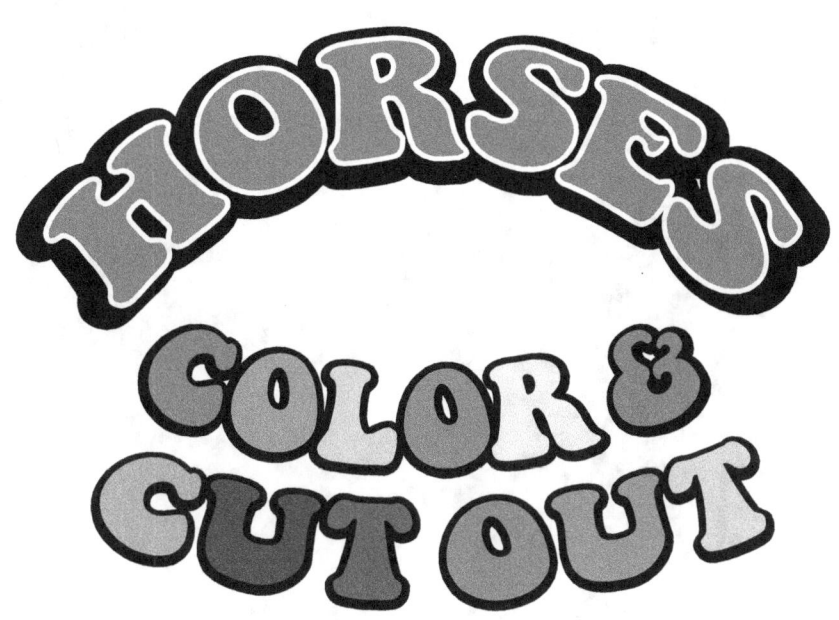

This coloring book belongs to:

_____

Copyright© 2021 Horses Color and Cut Out

All rights reserved.
No part of this book may be reprinted or reproduced or utilized in any form or by any electronic, mechanical, or other means, now known or hereafter invented, including photocopying and recording, or in any information storage or retrieval system without permission in writing from the publishers.

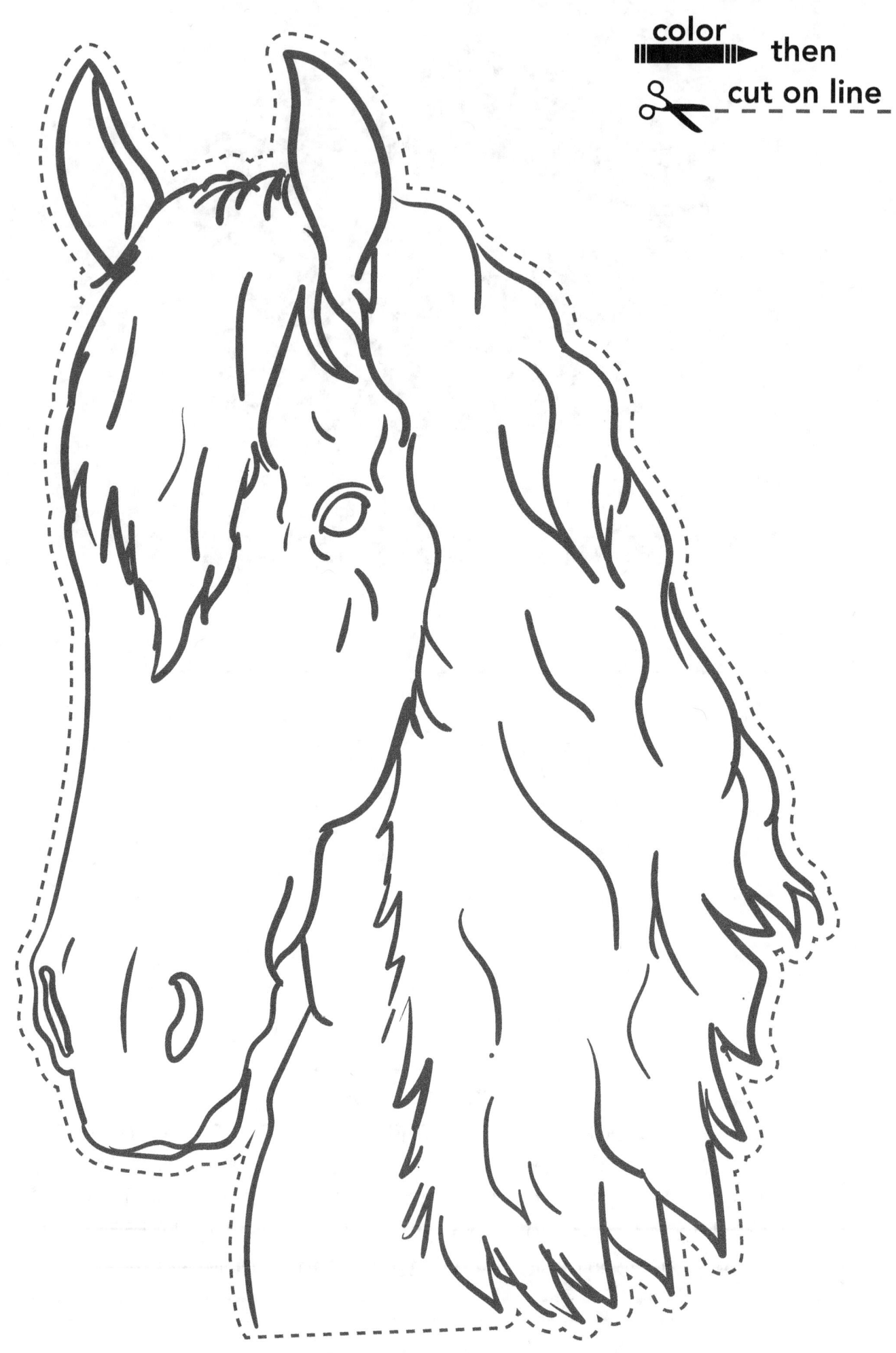

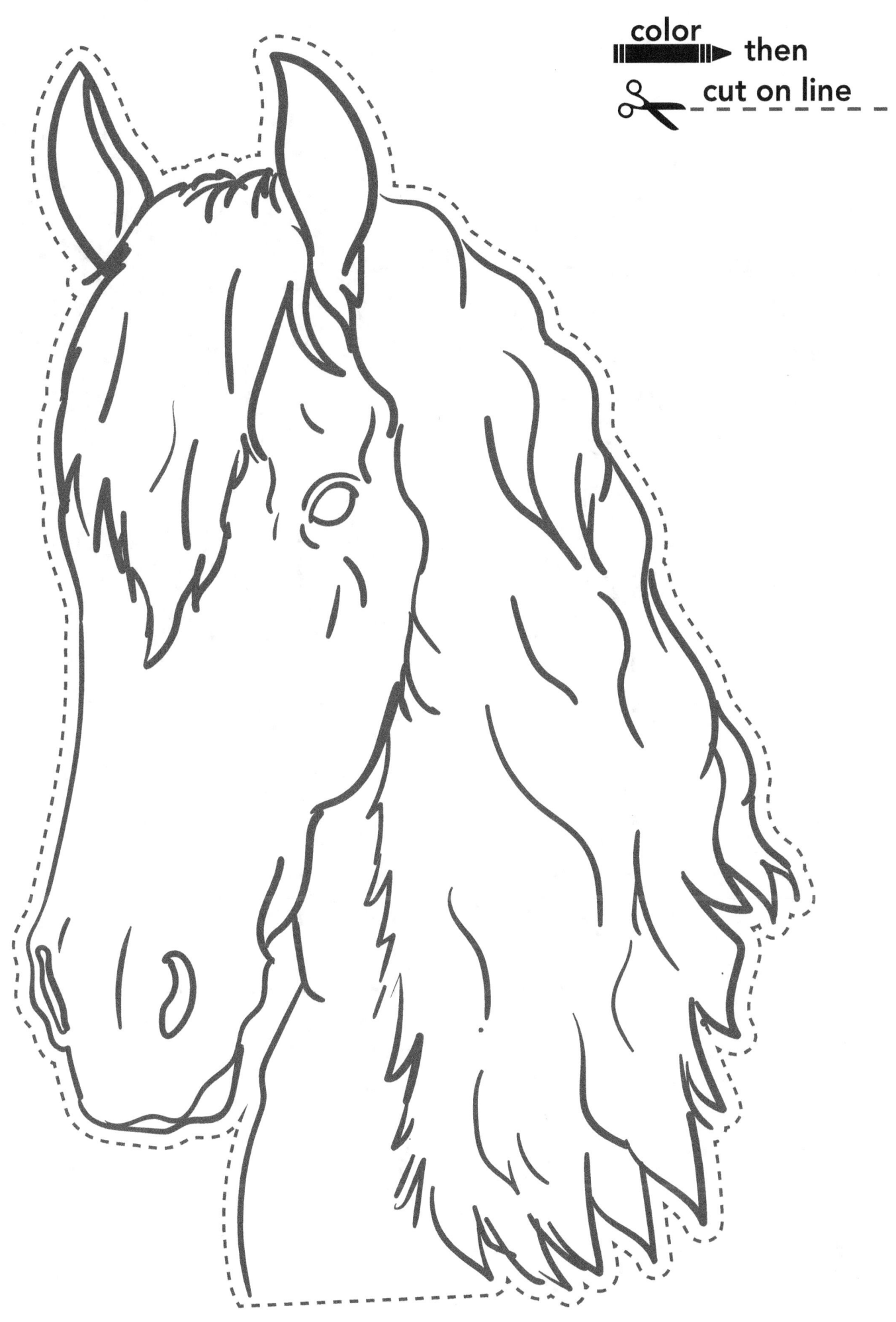

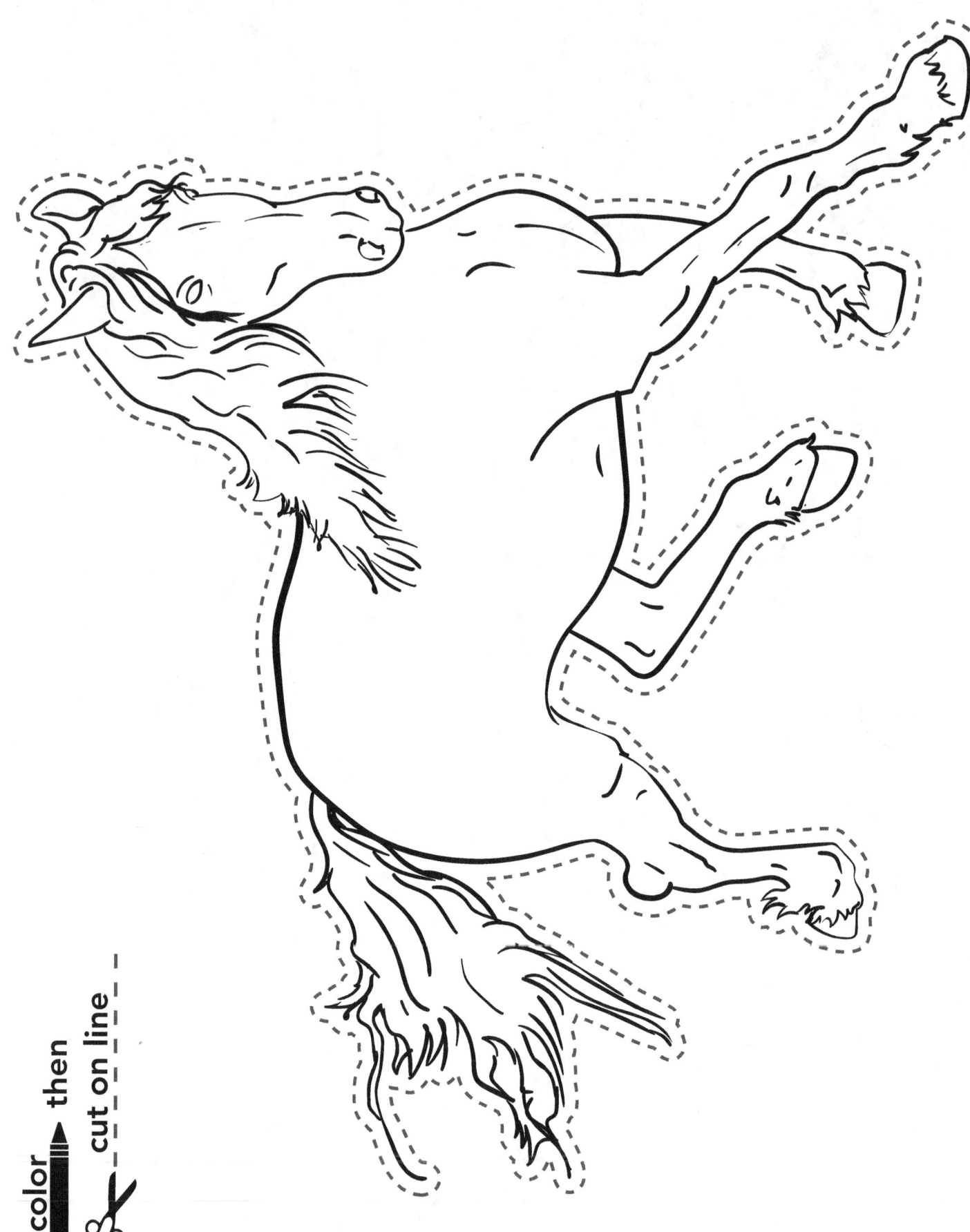

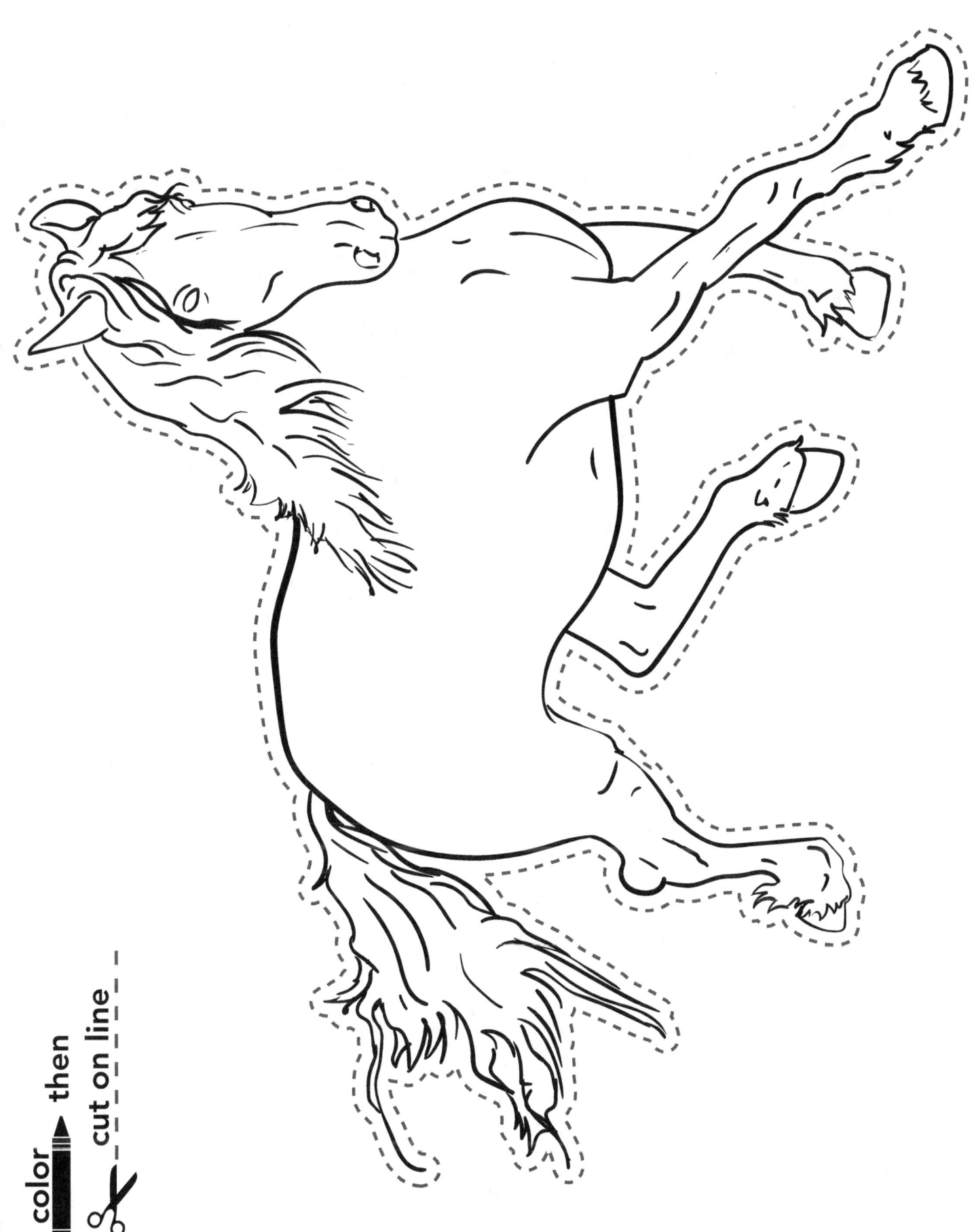

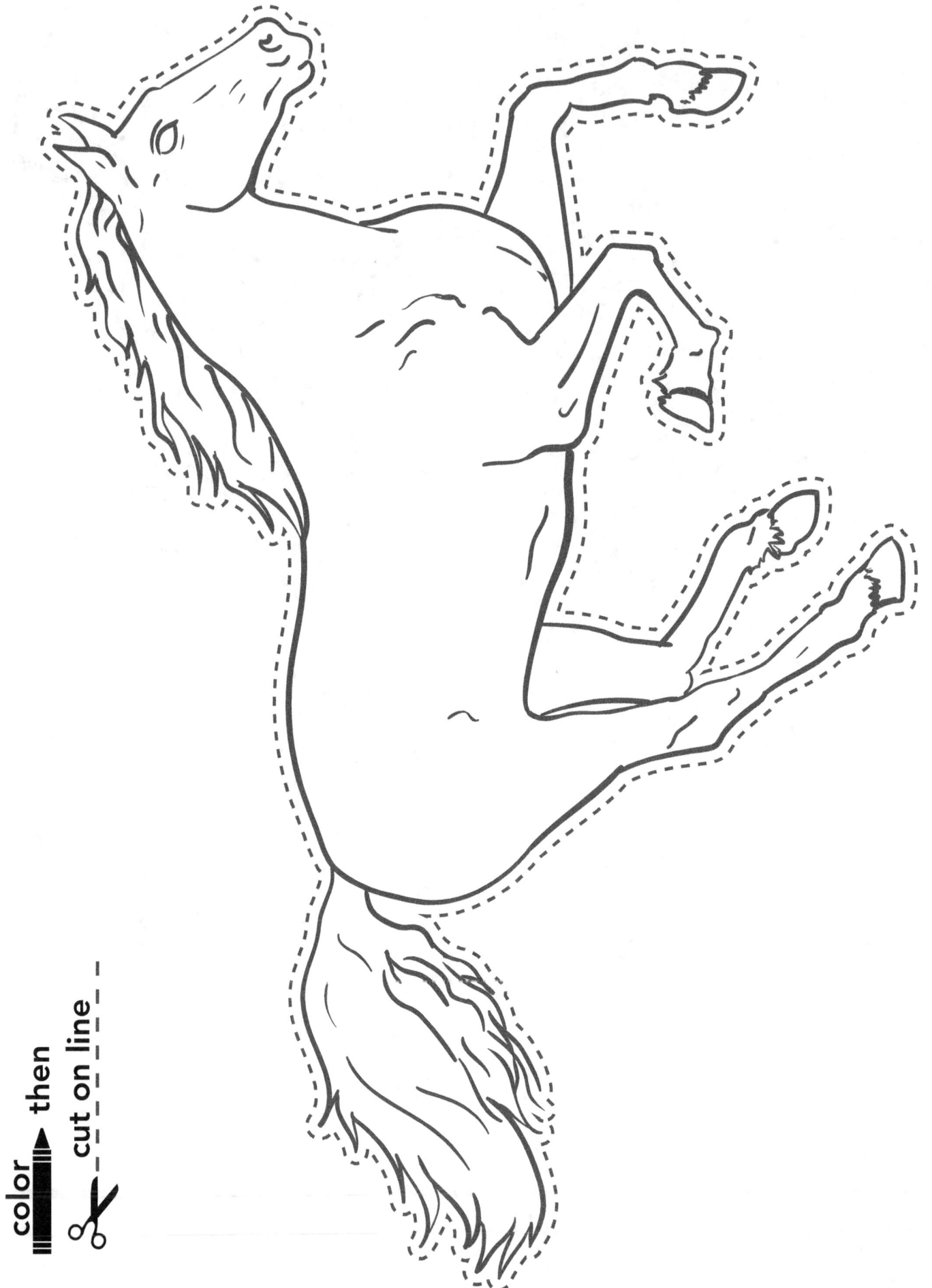

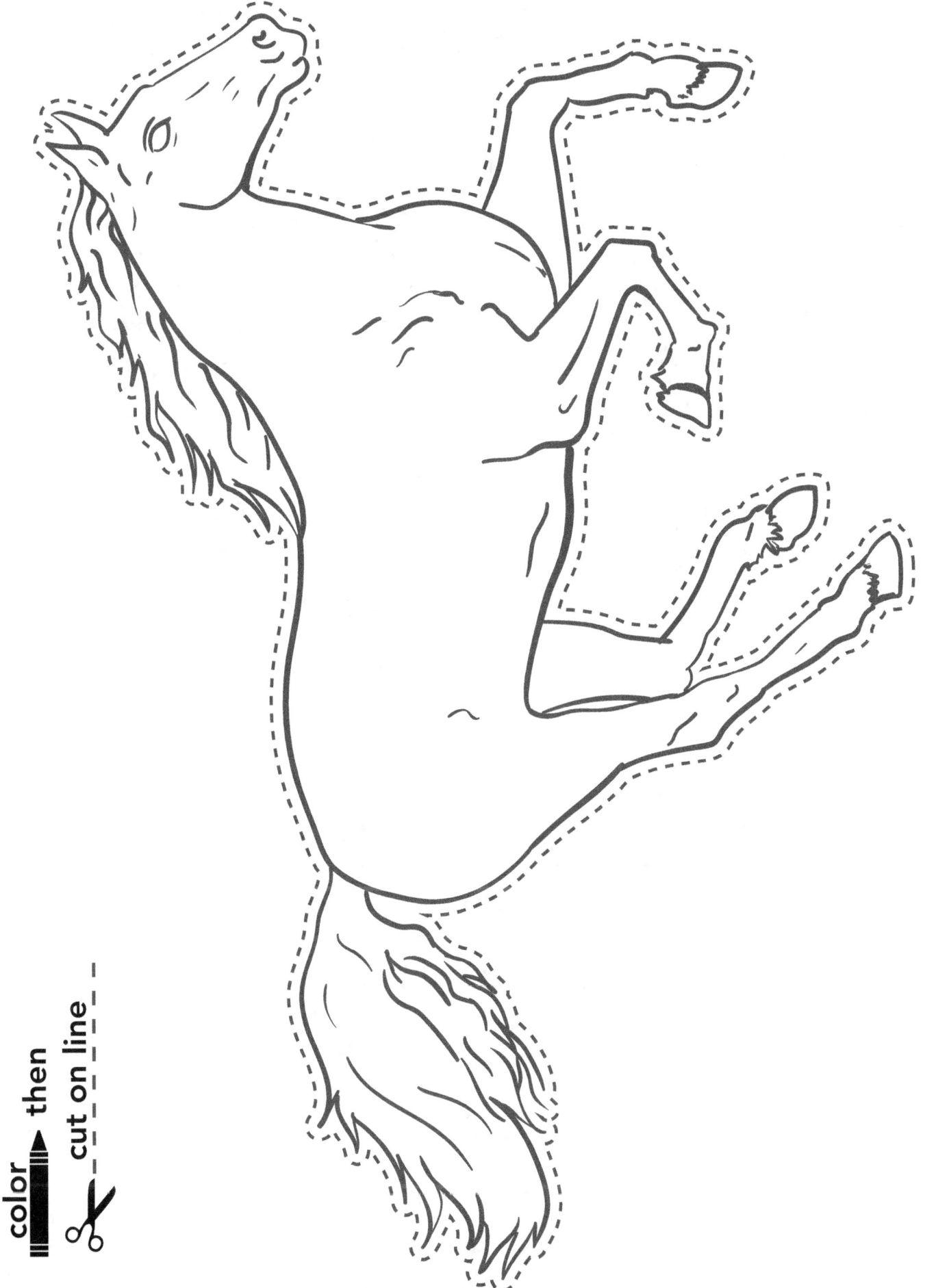

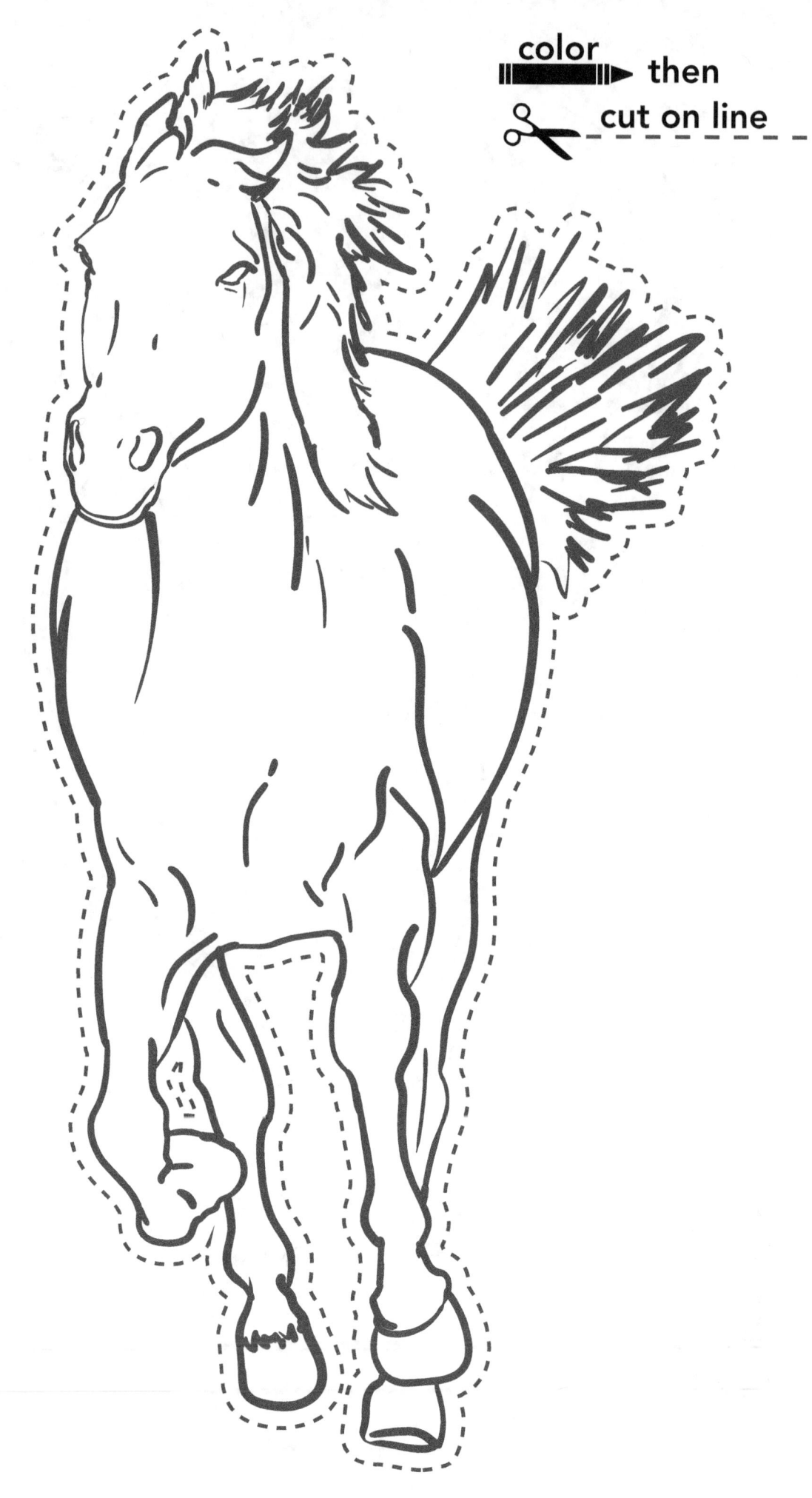

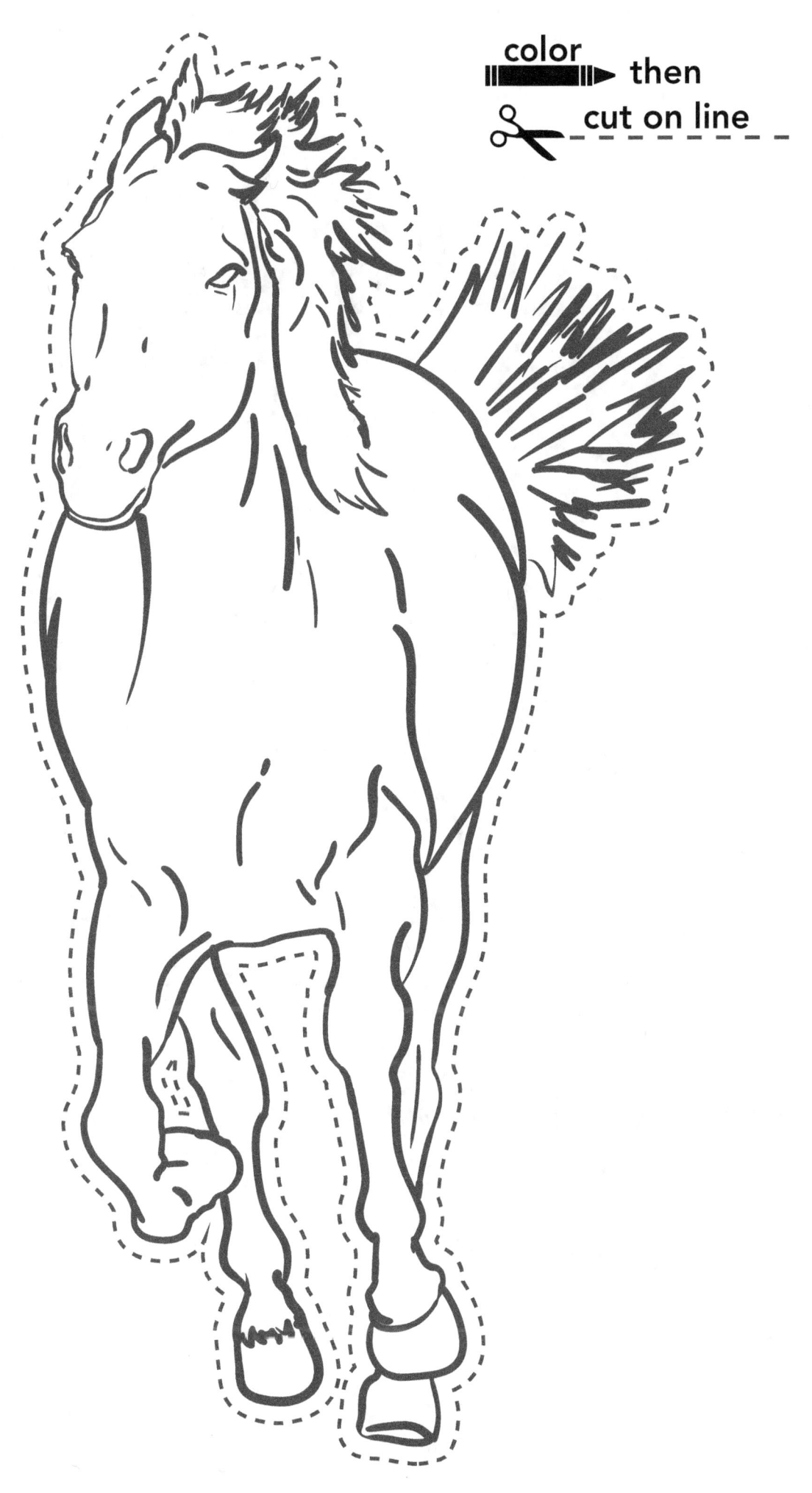

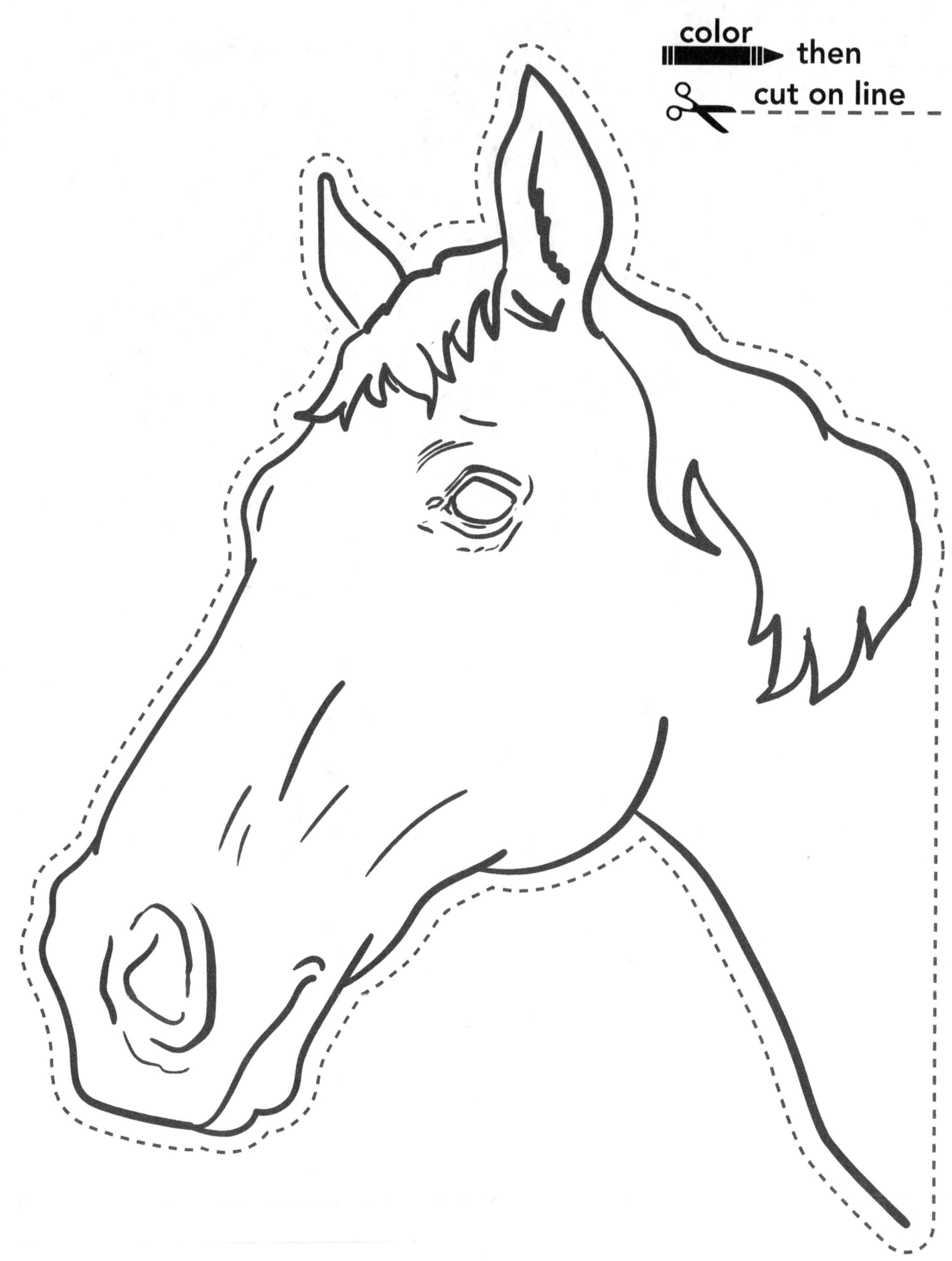

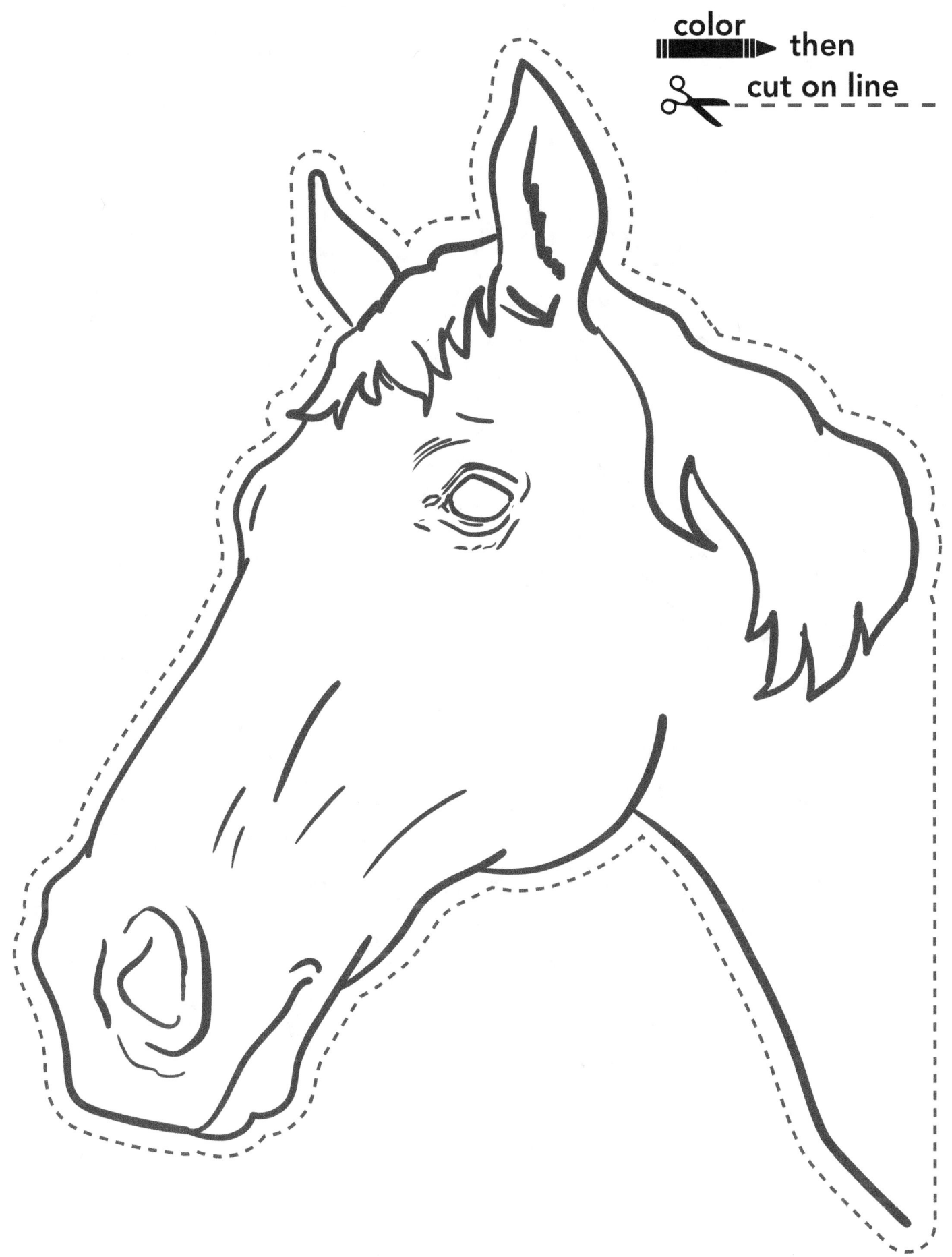

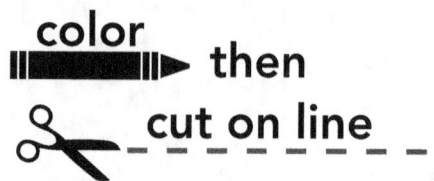

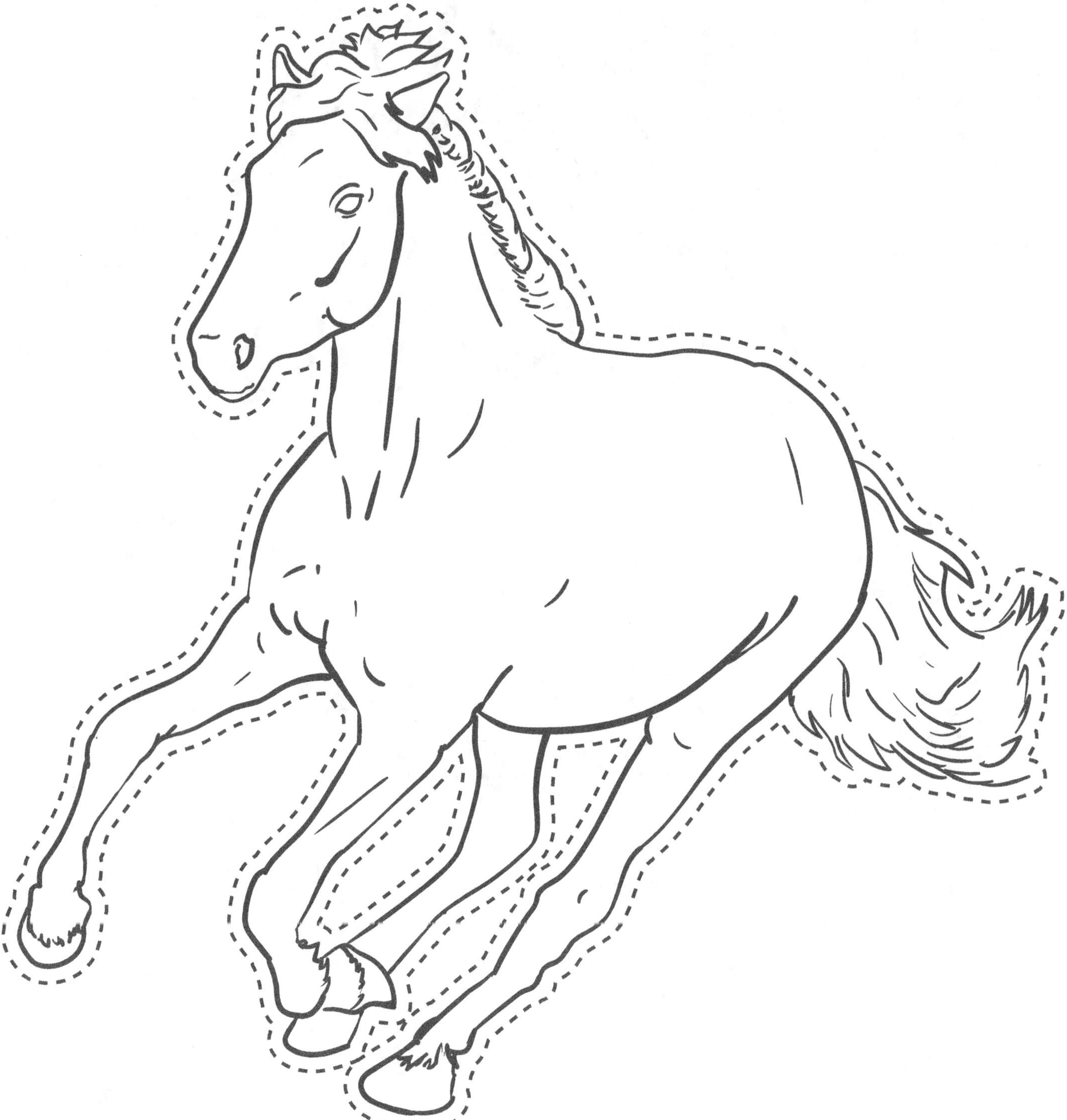

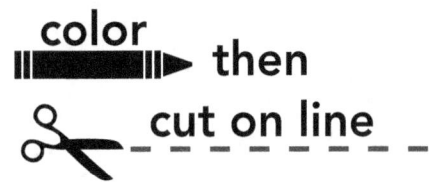
color then cut on line

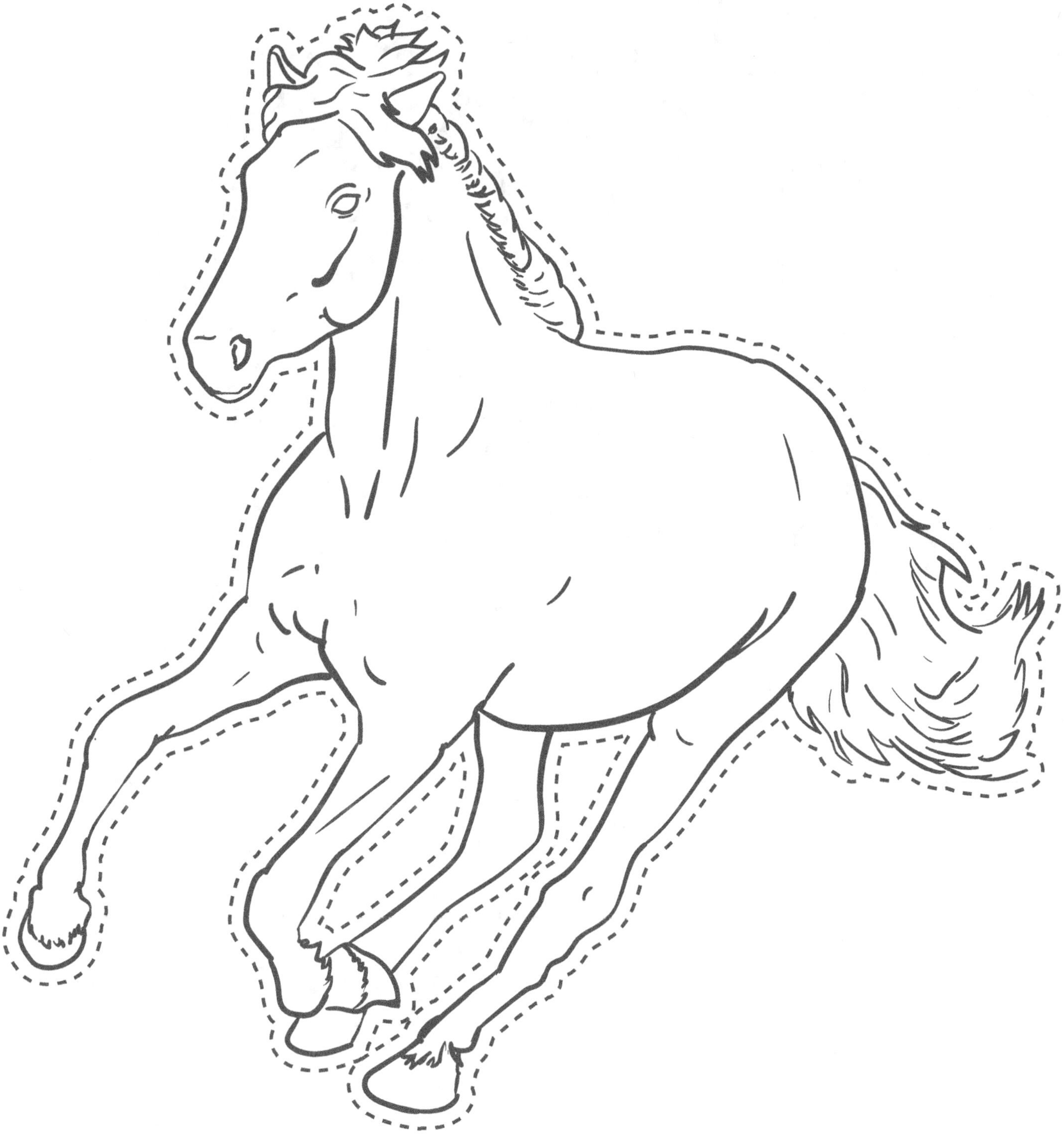

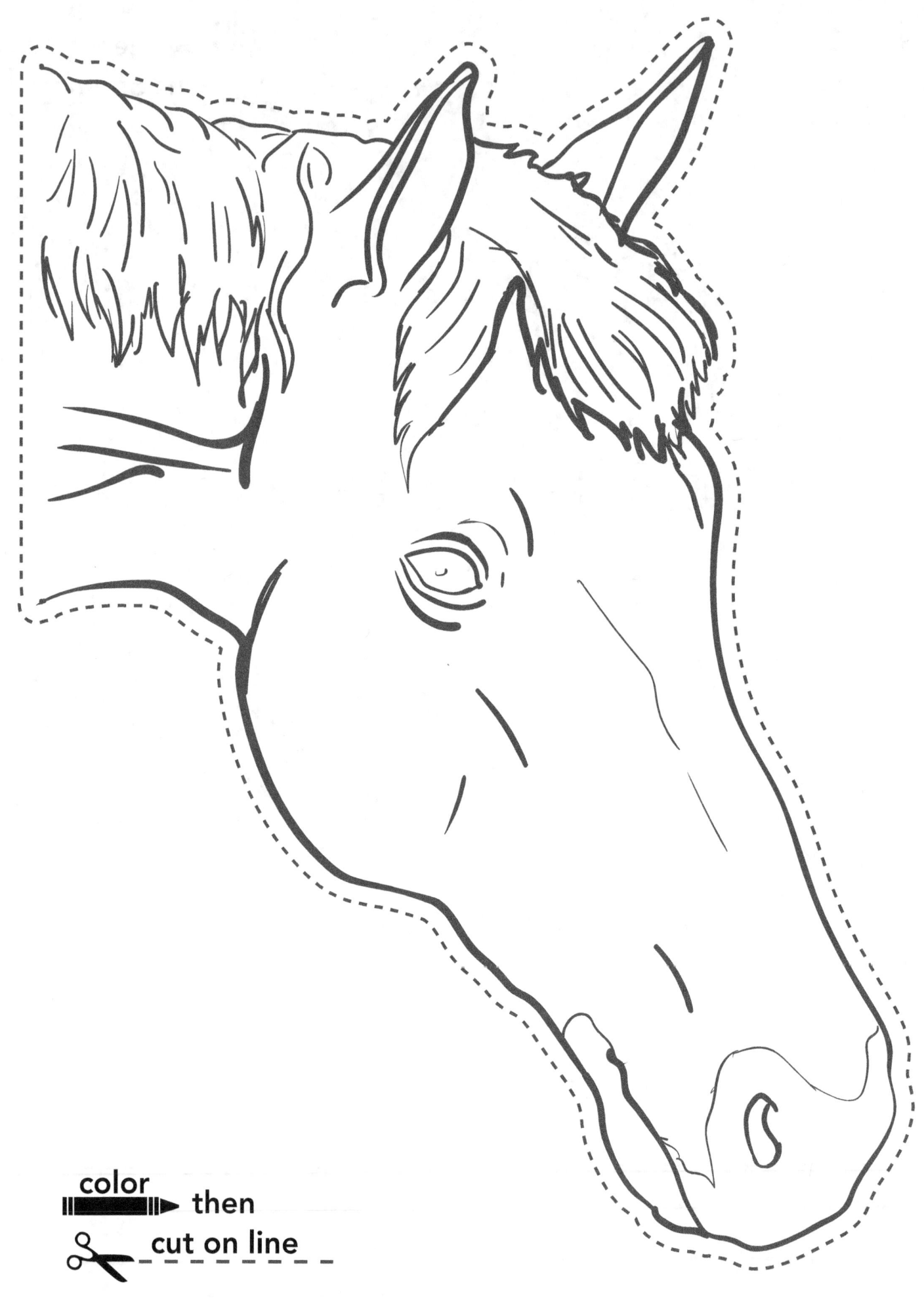

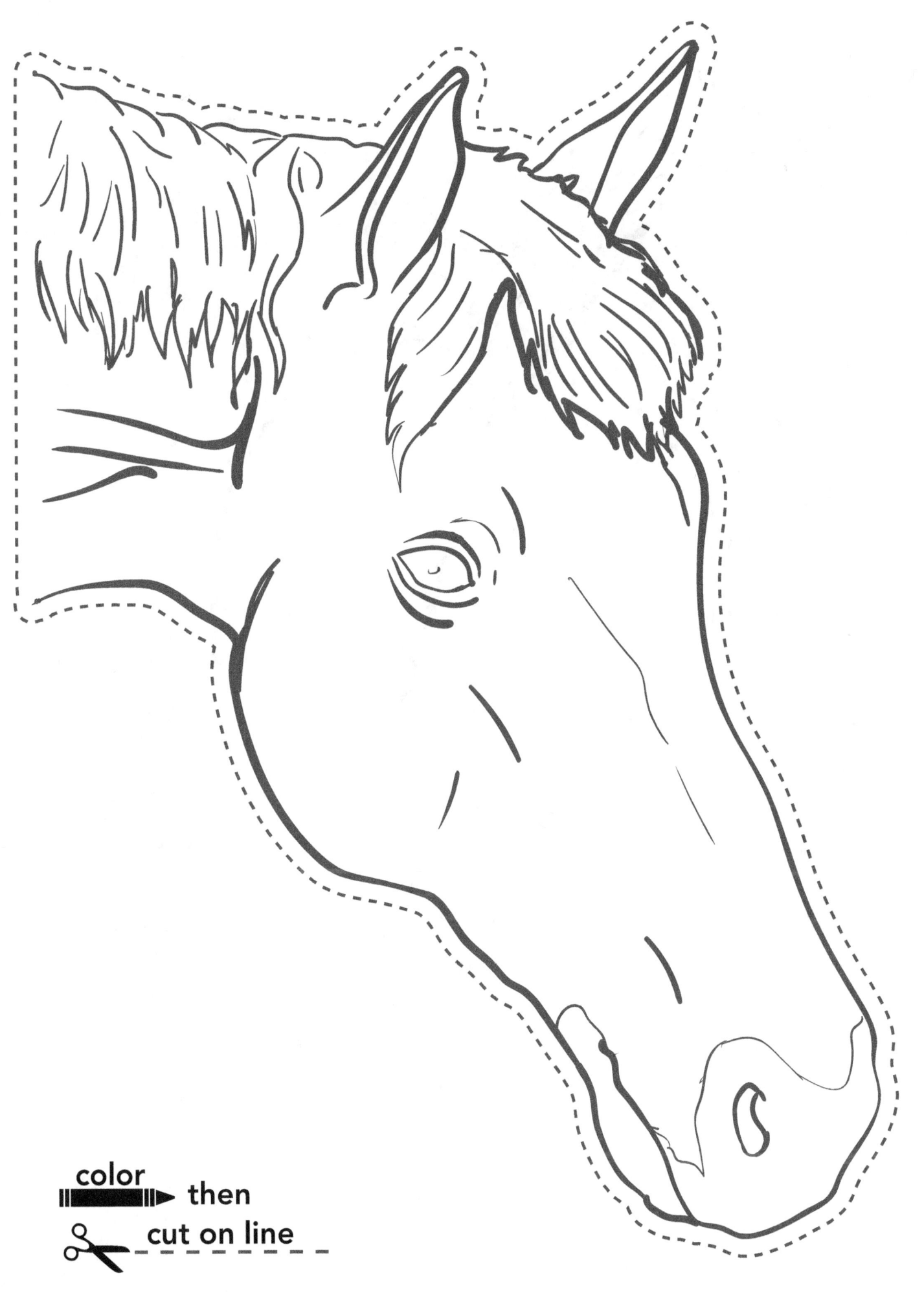

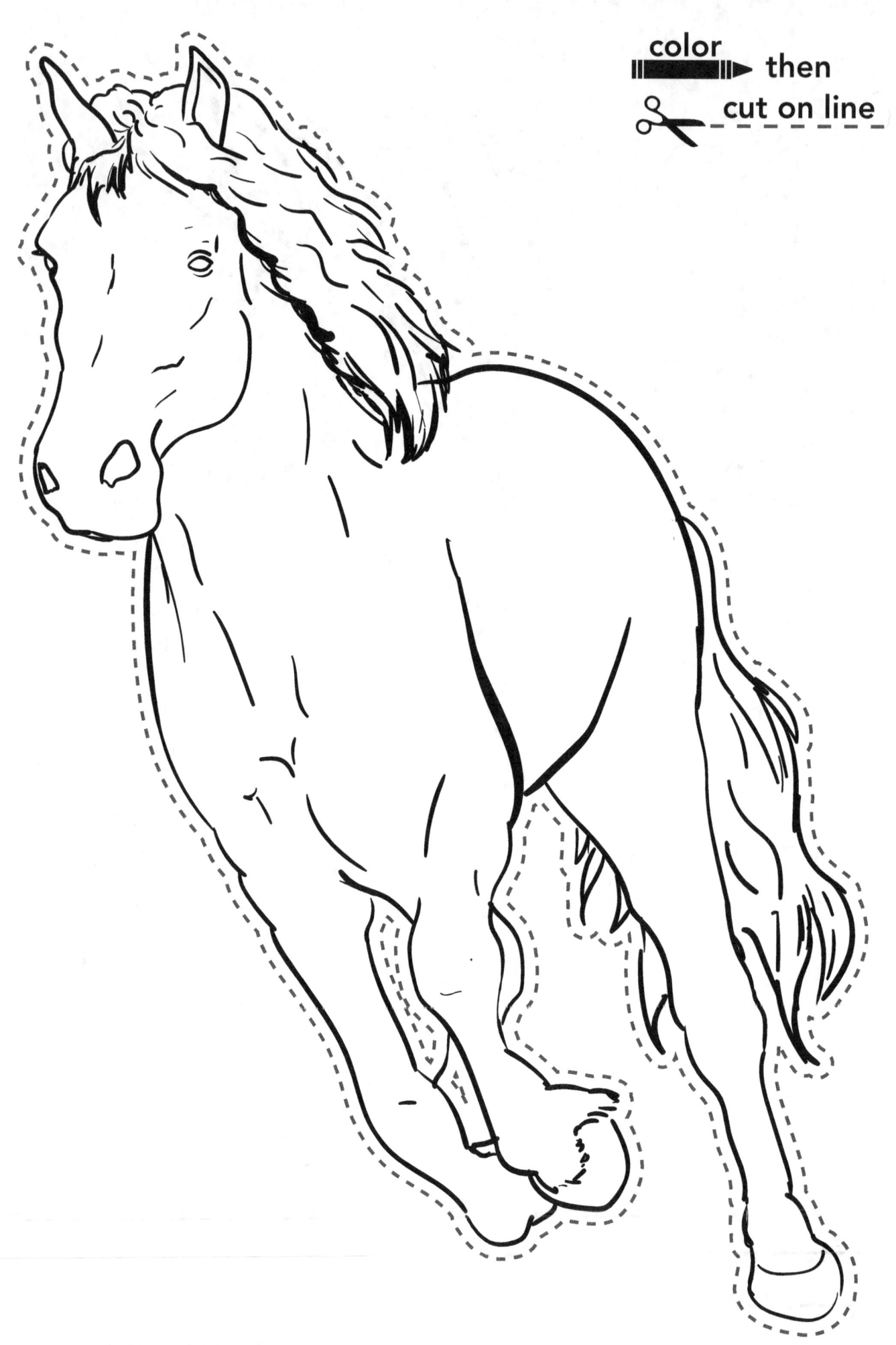

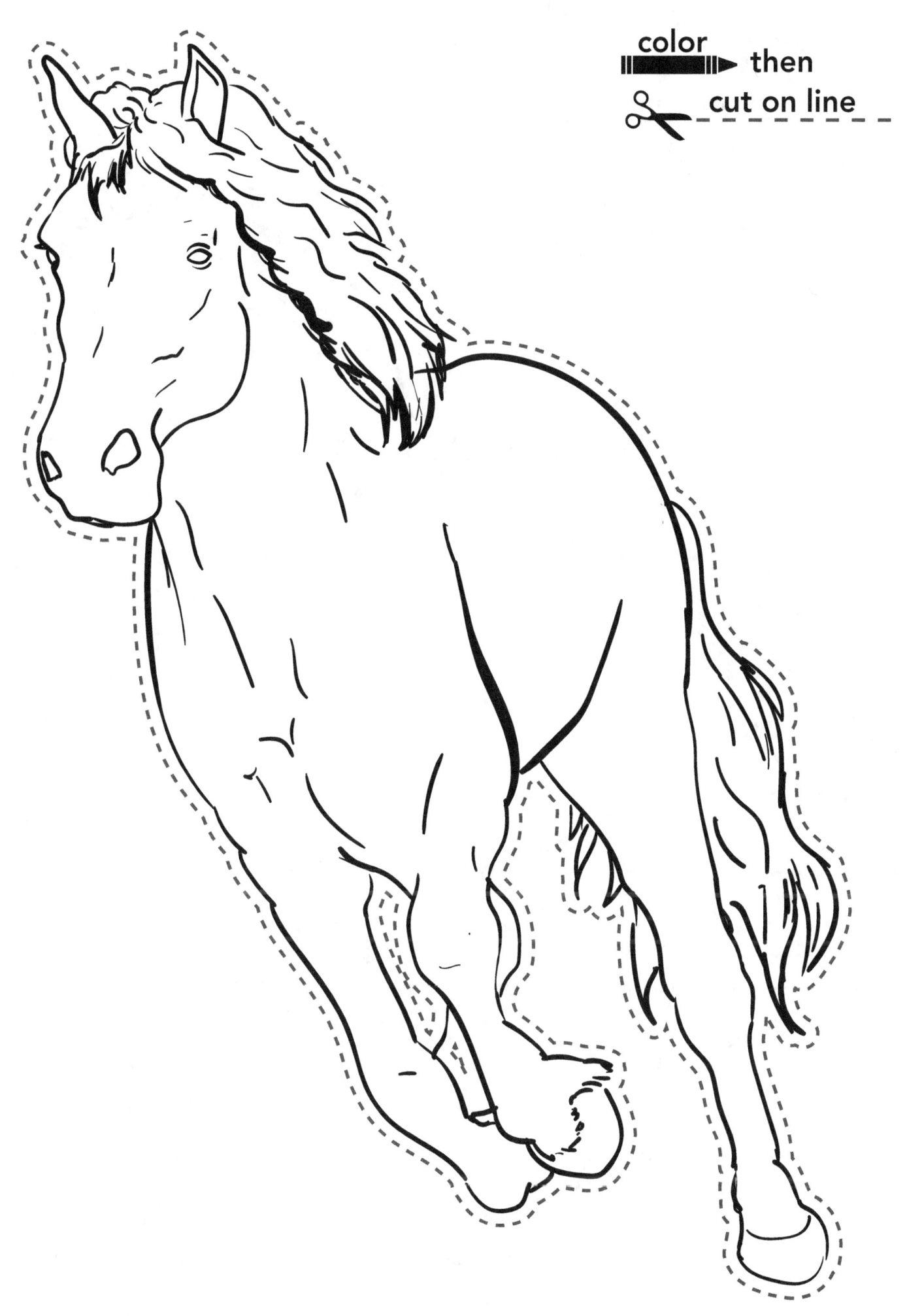

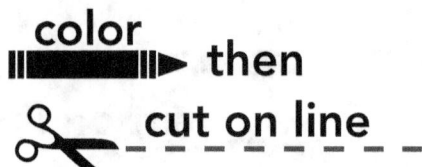

color then cut on line

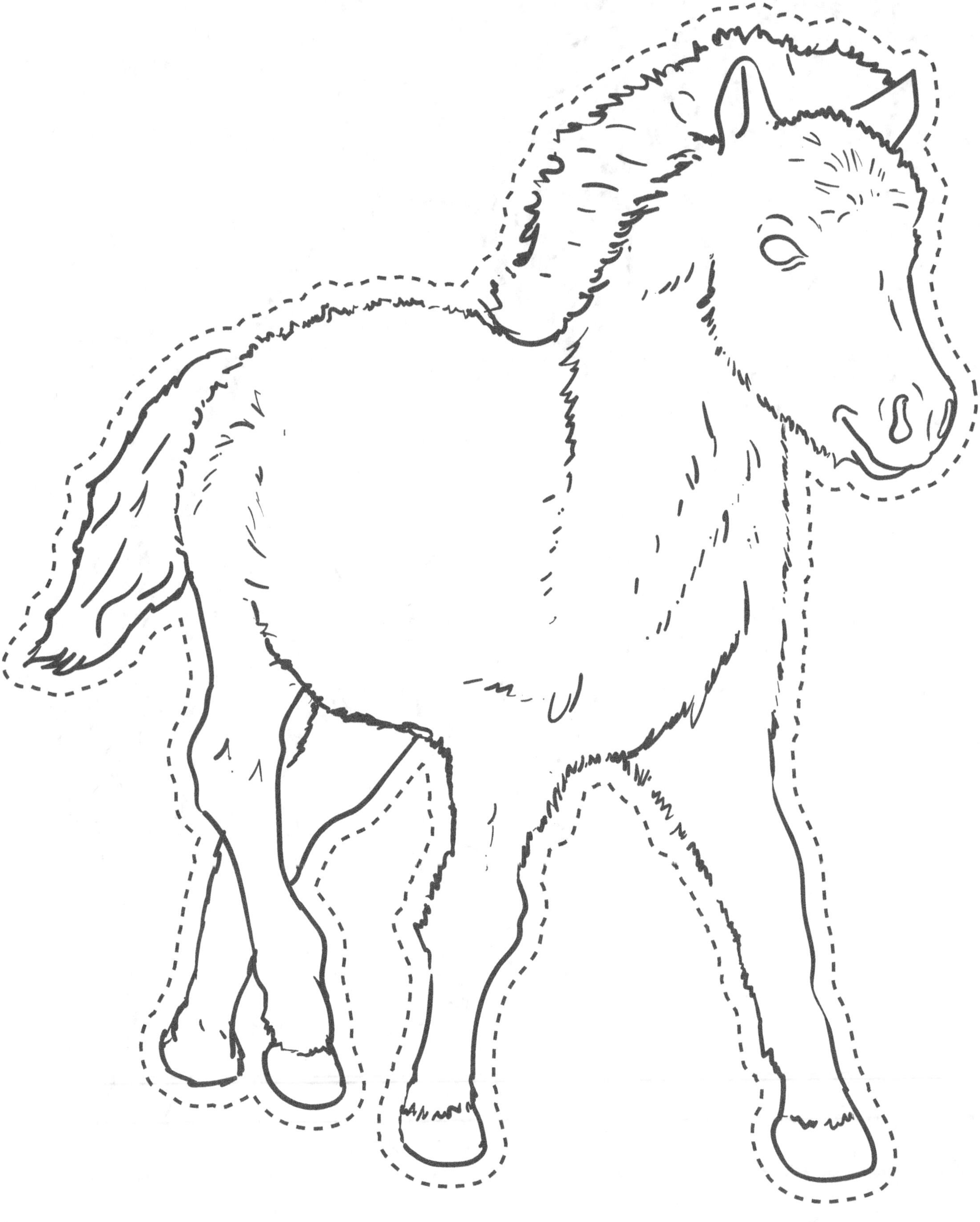

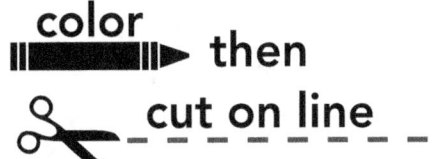

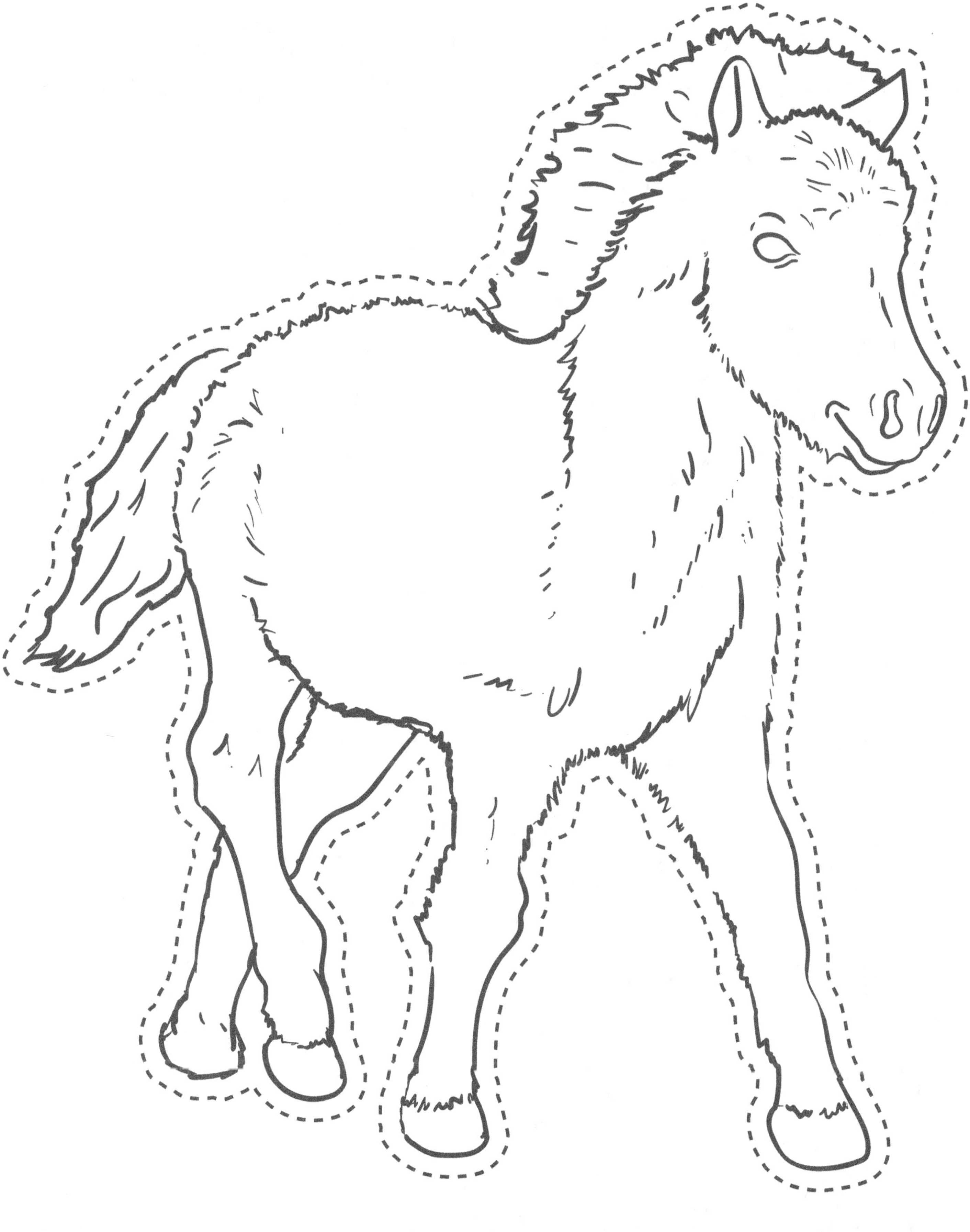

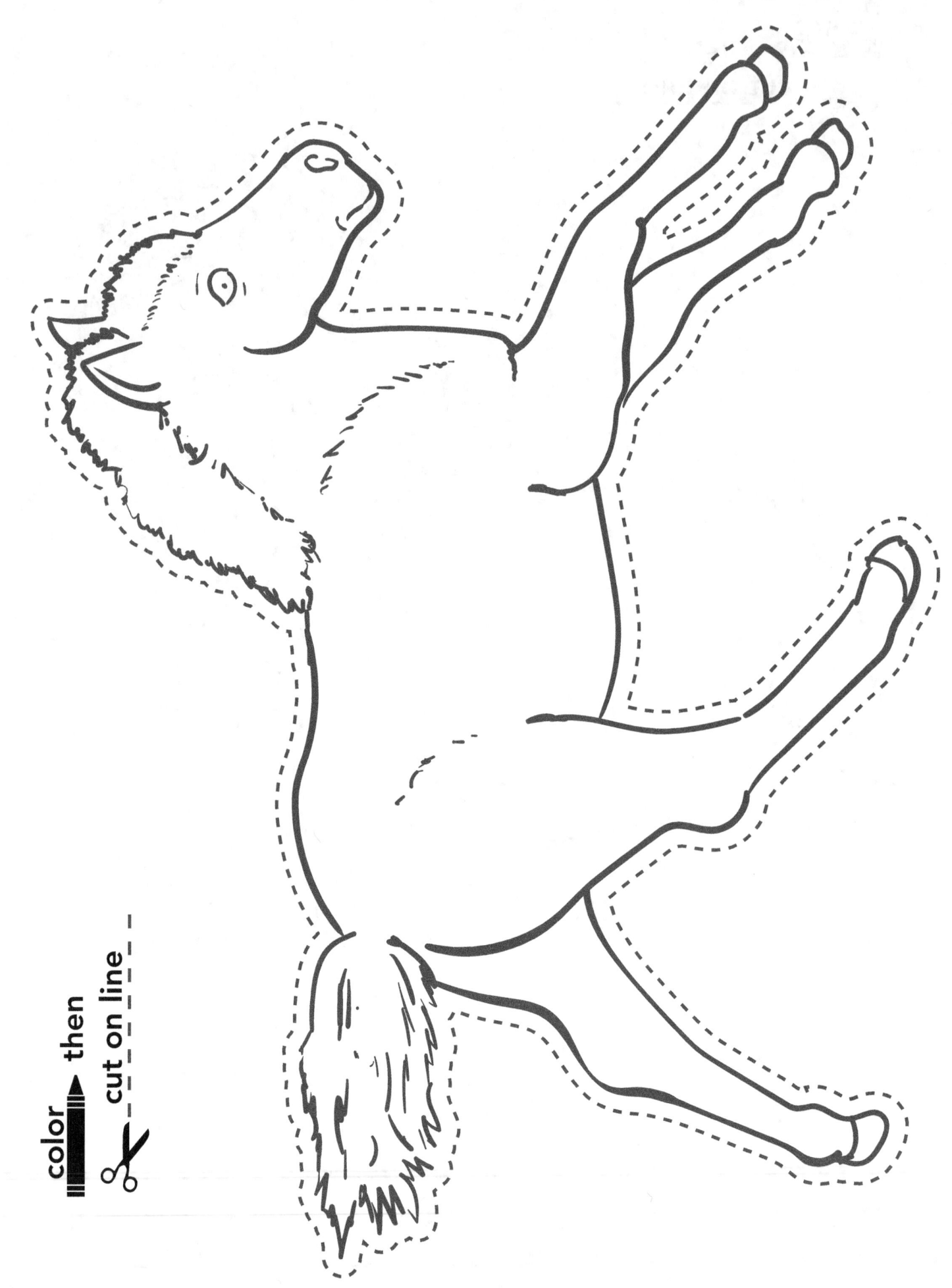

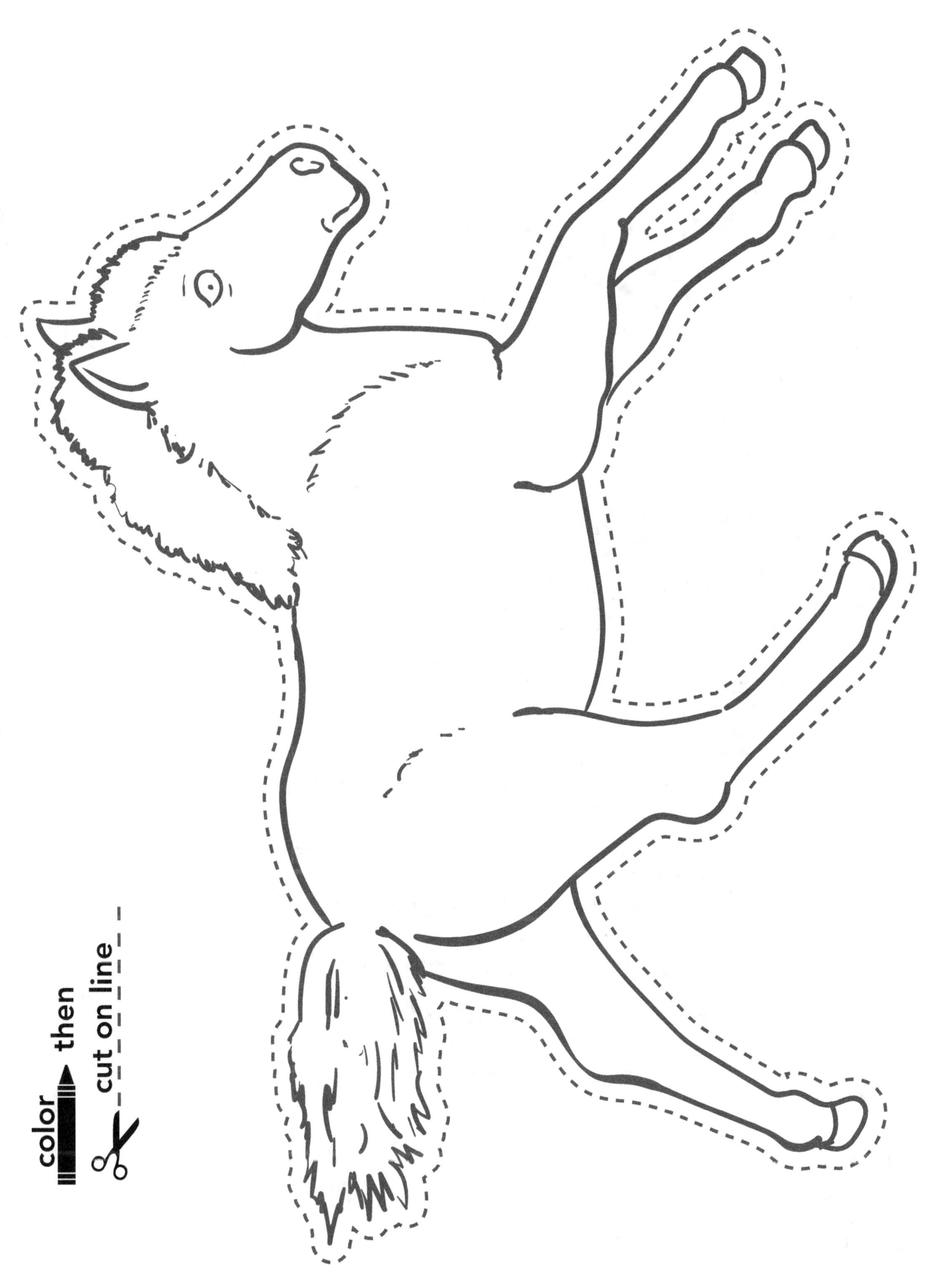

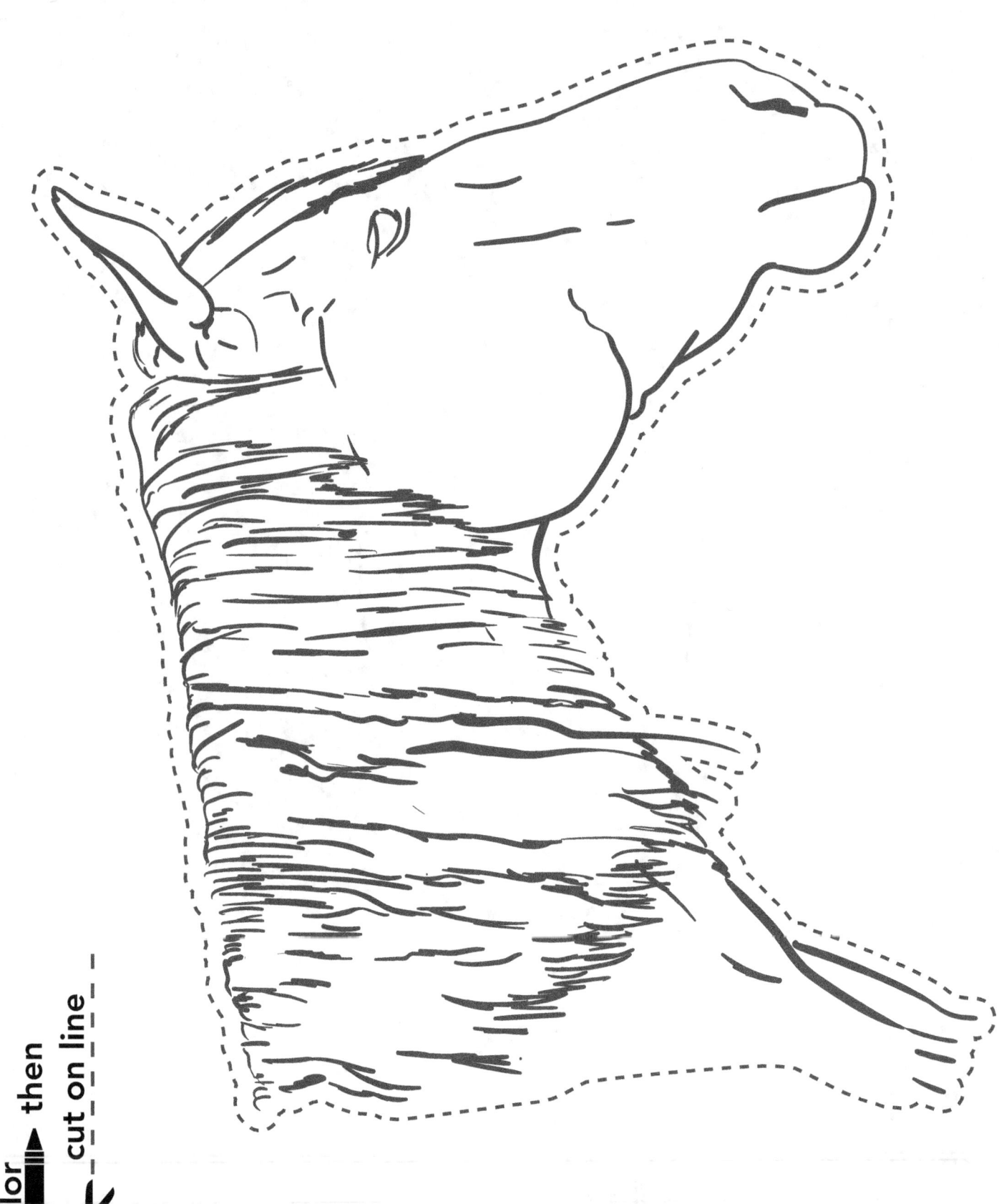

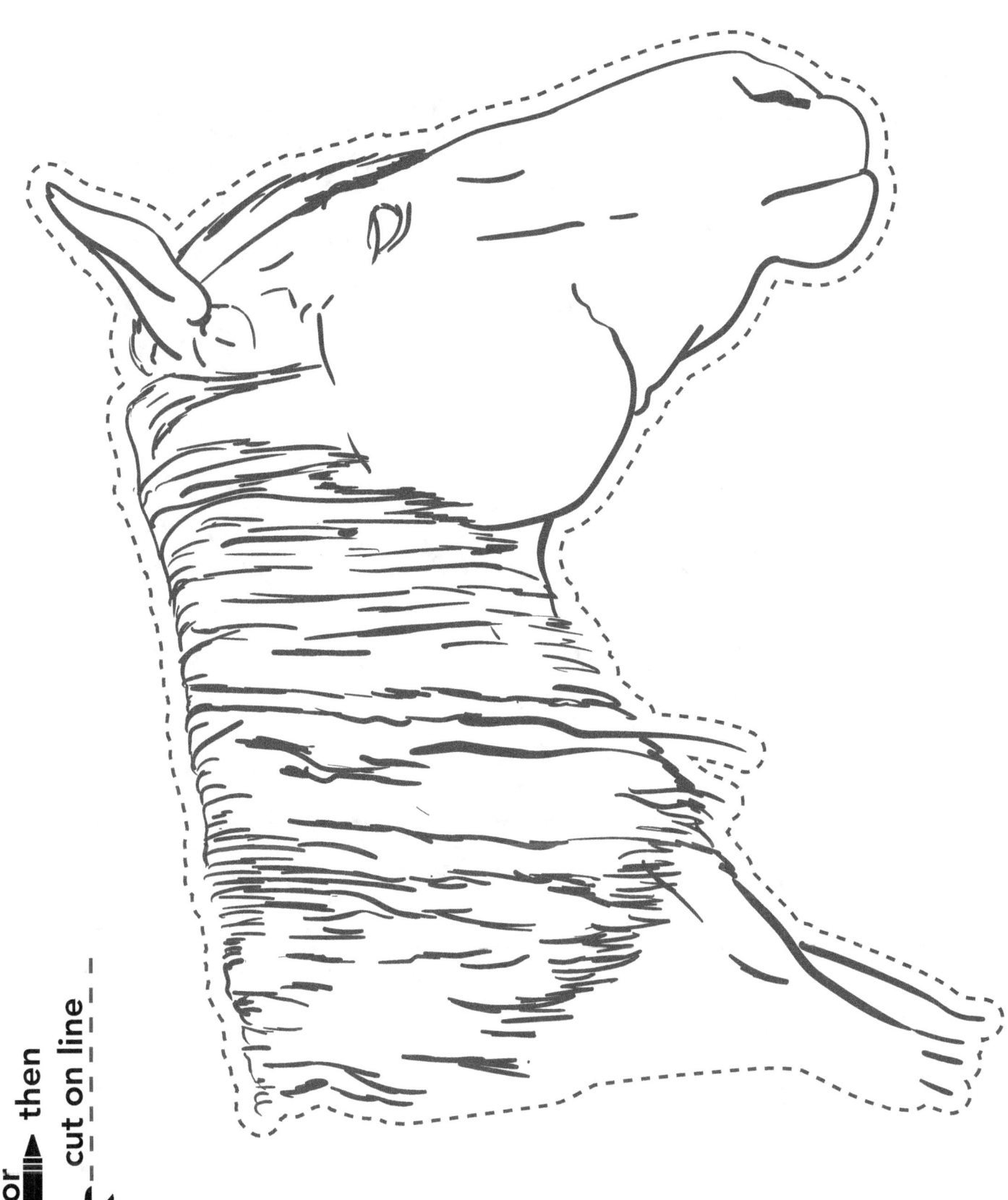

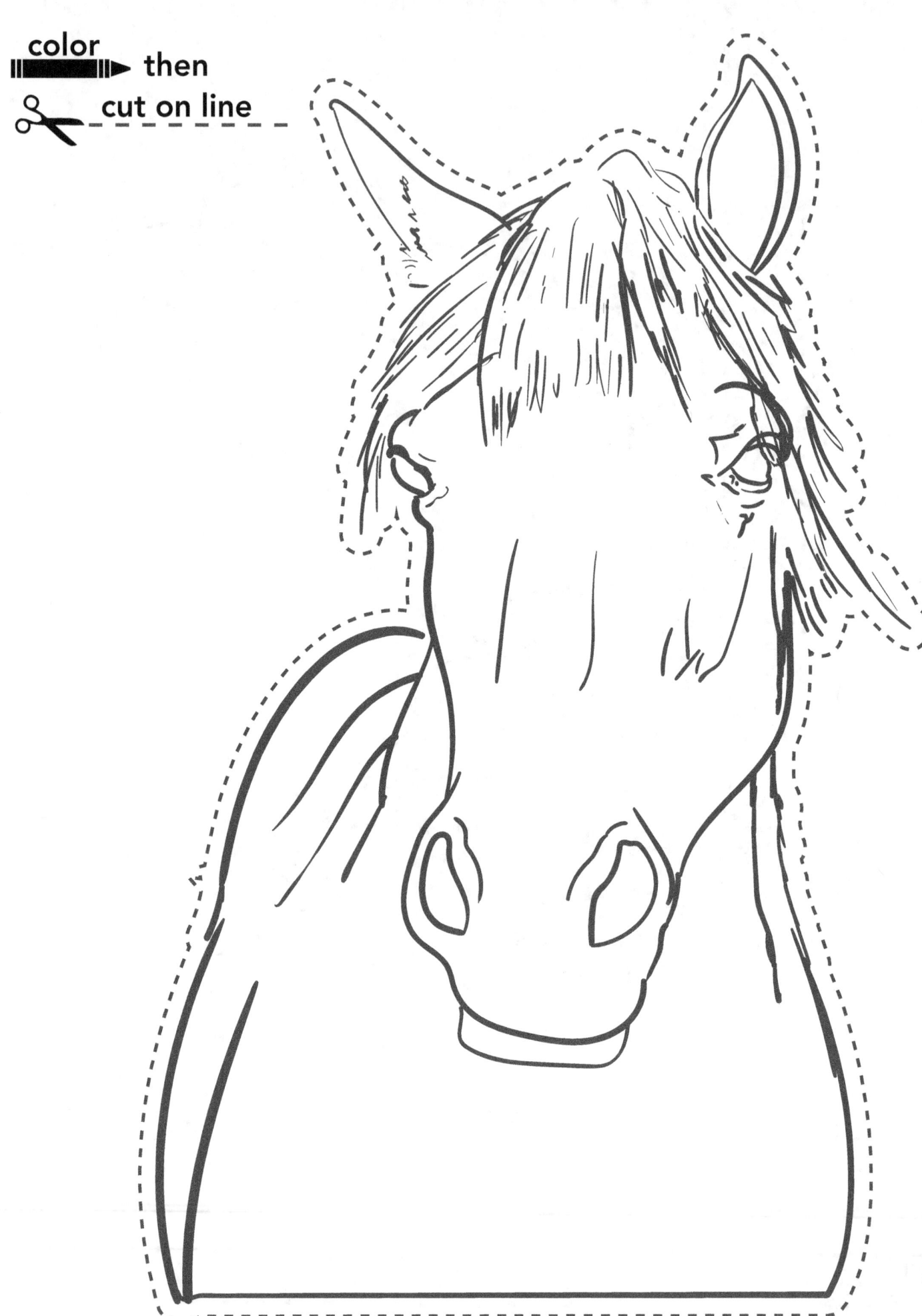

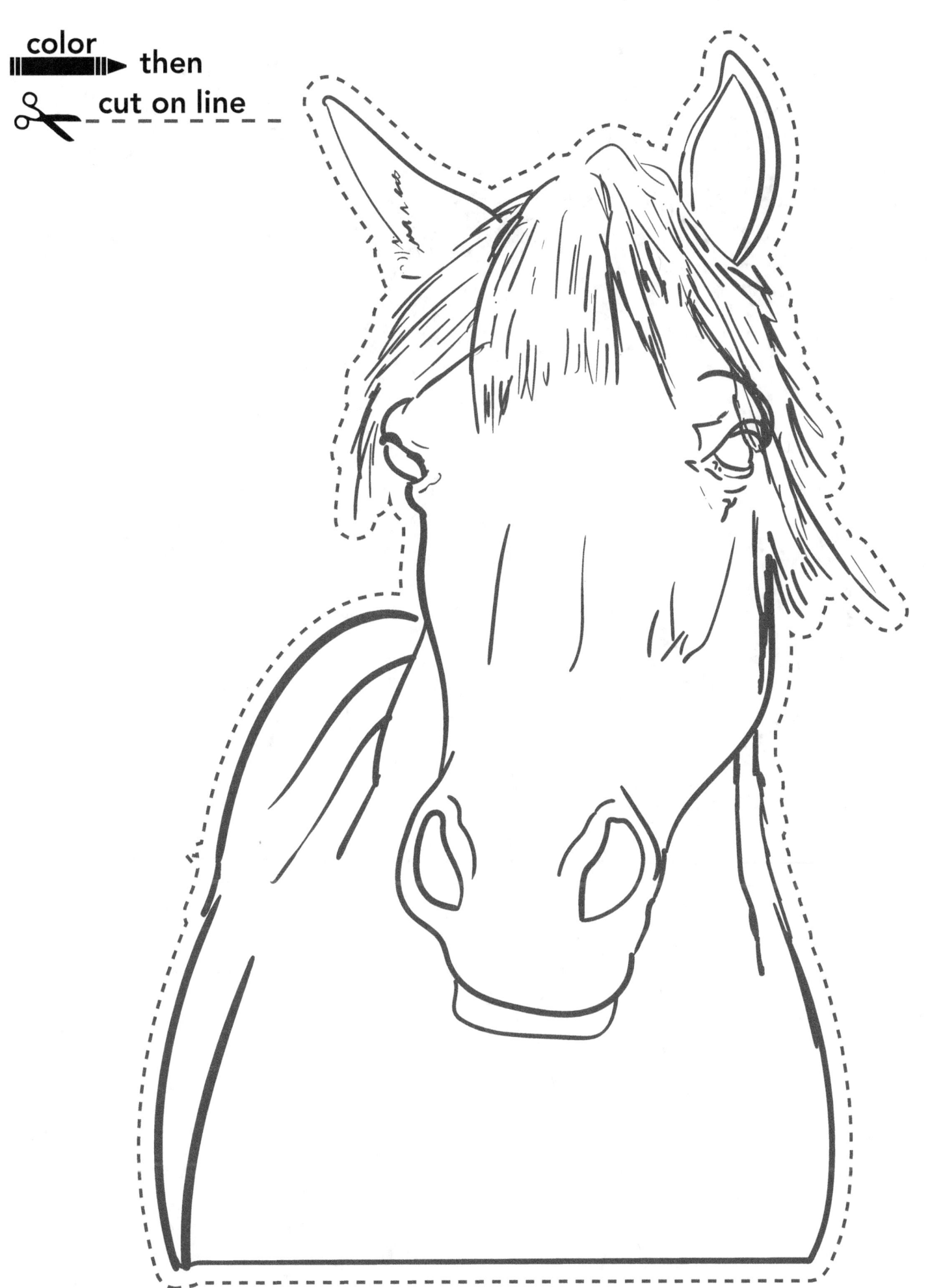

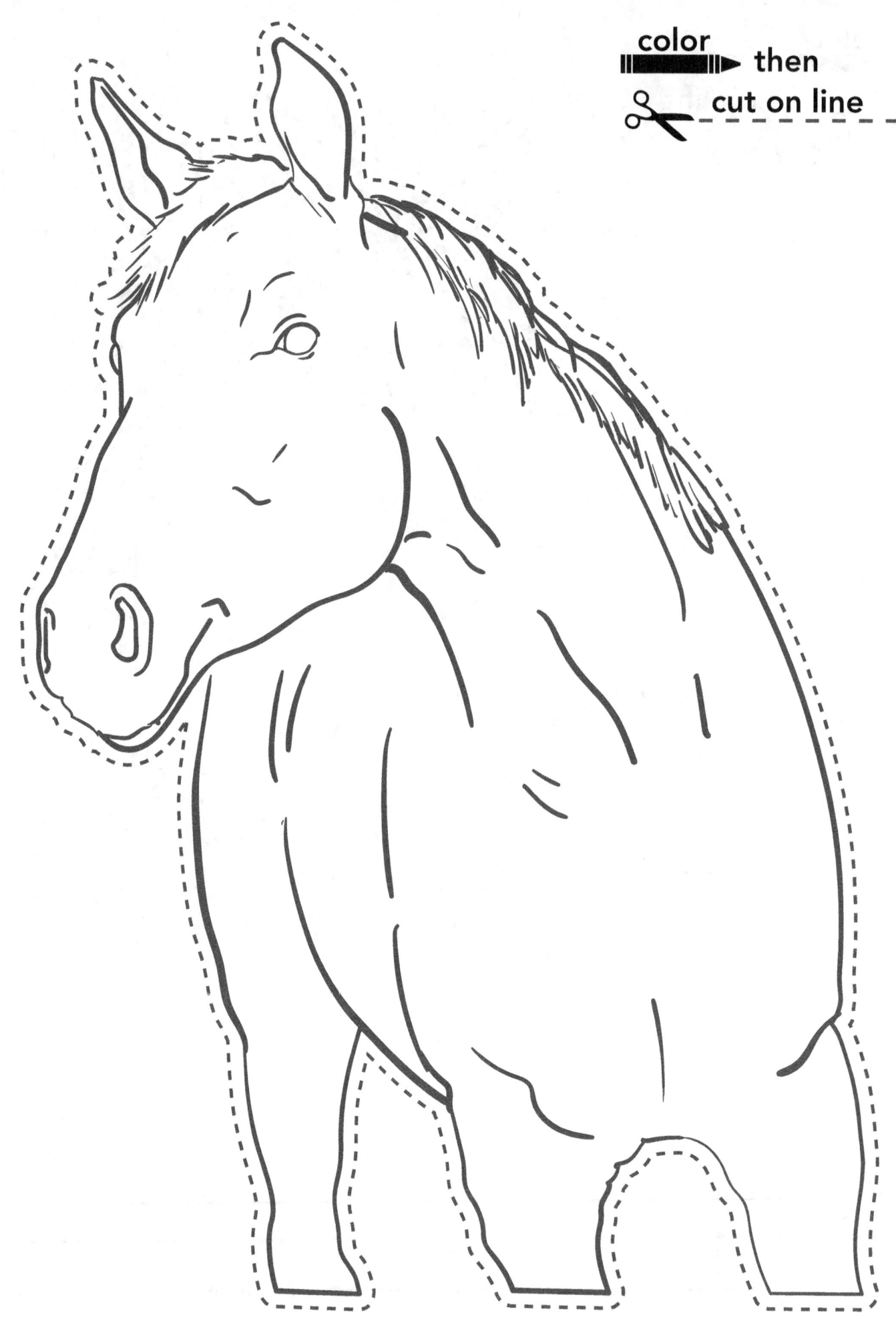

color then cut on line

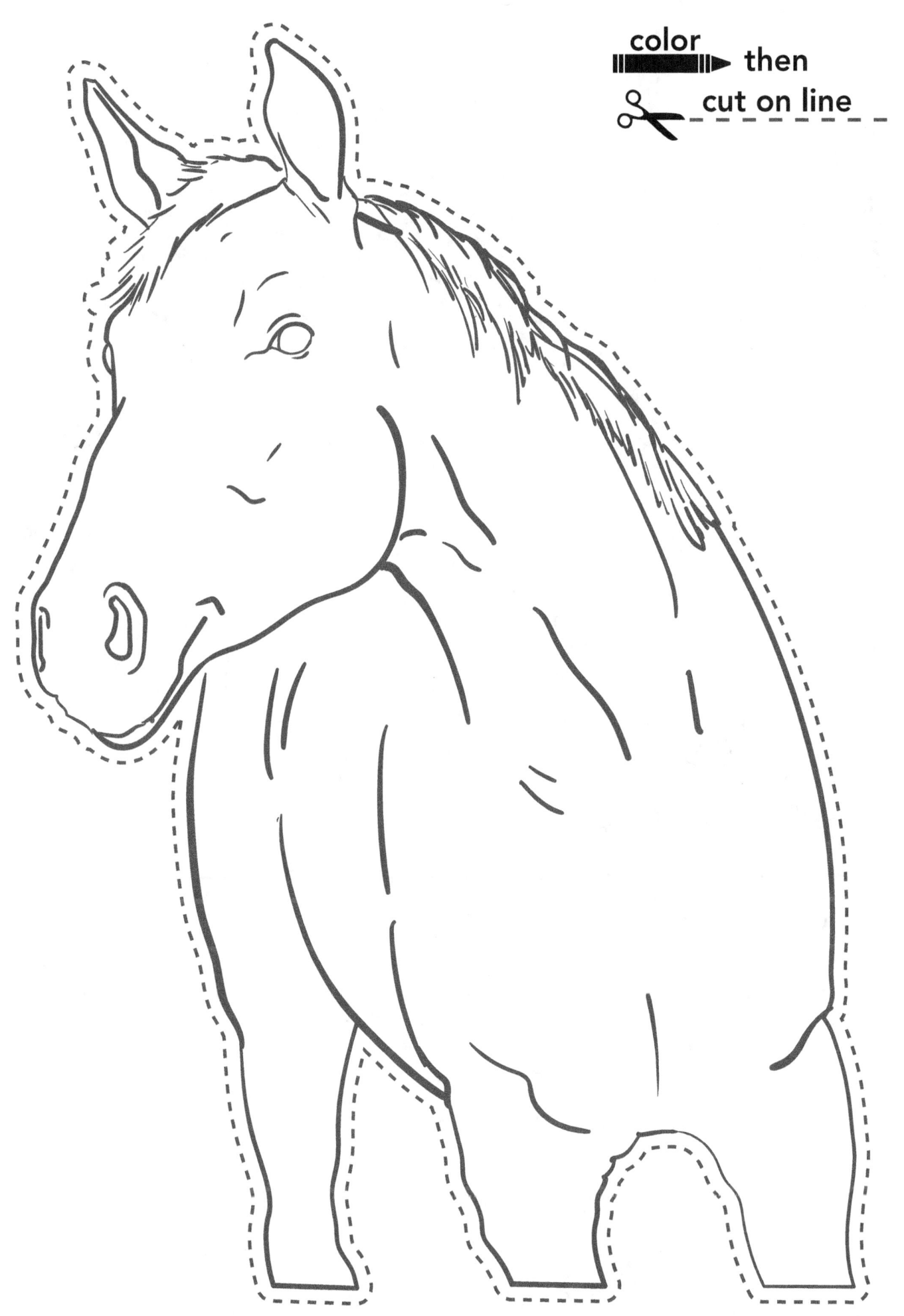

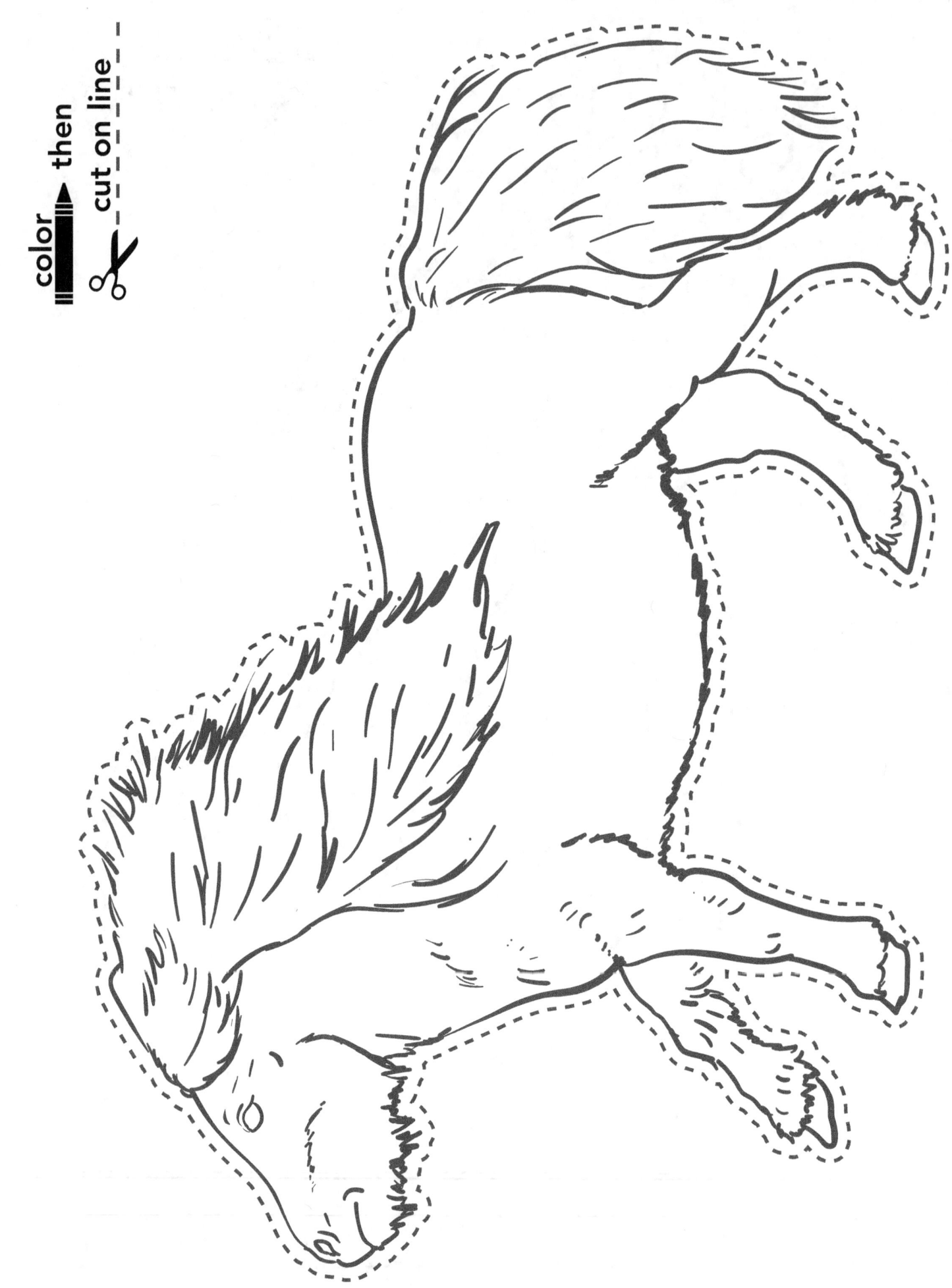

color then cut on line

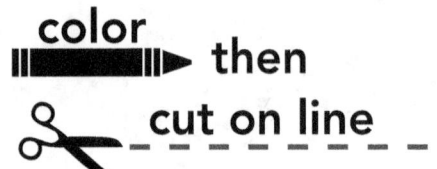

color then cut on line

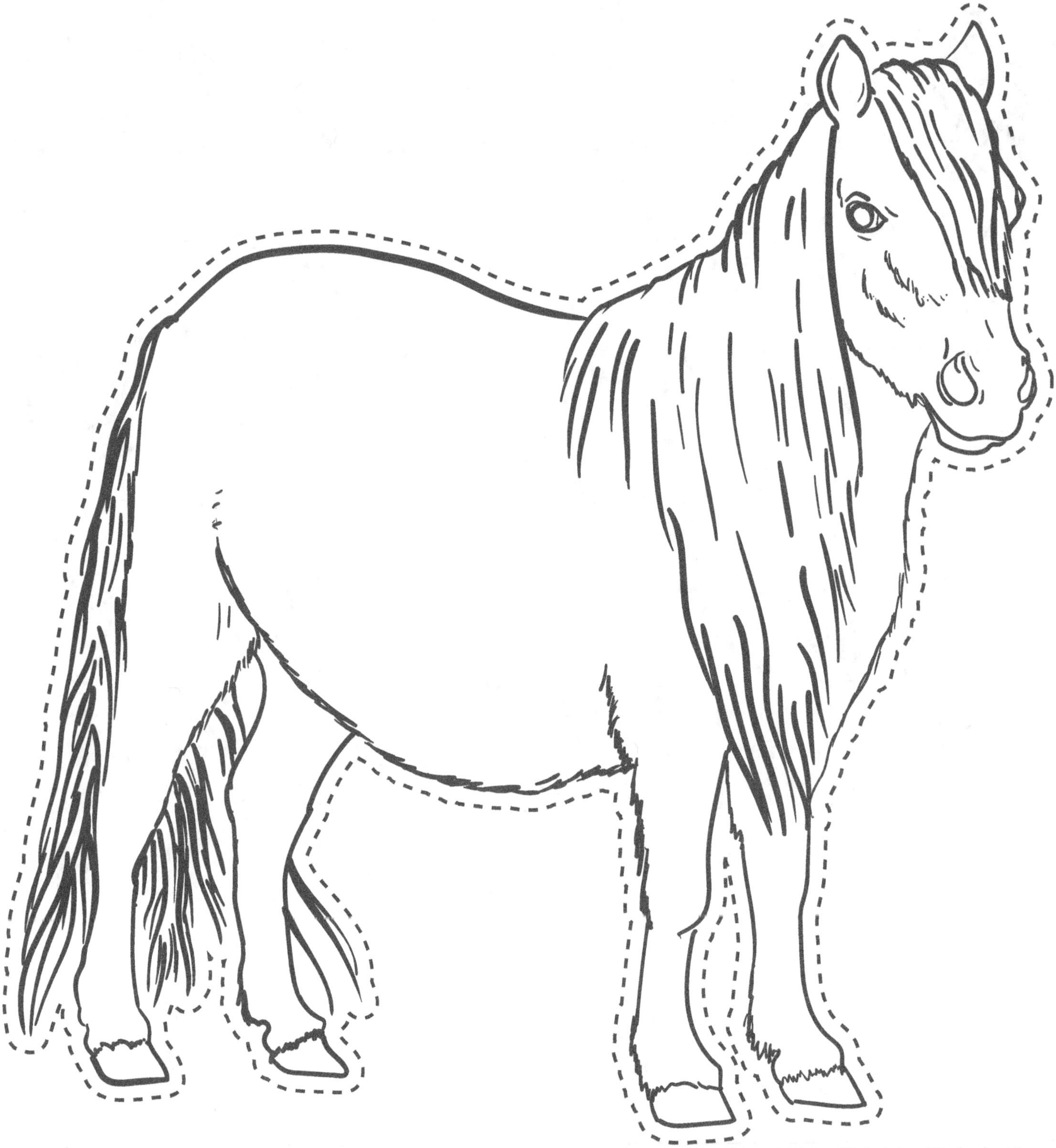

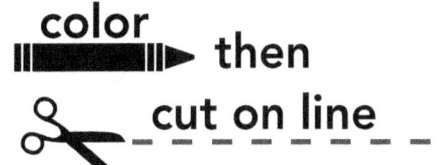

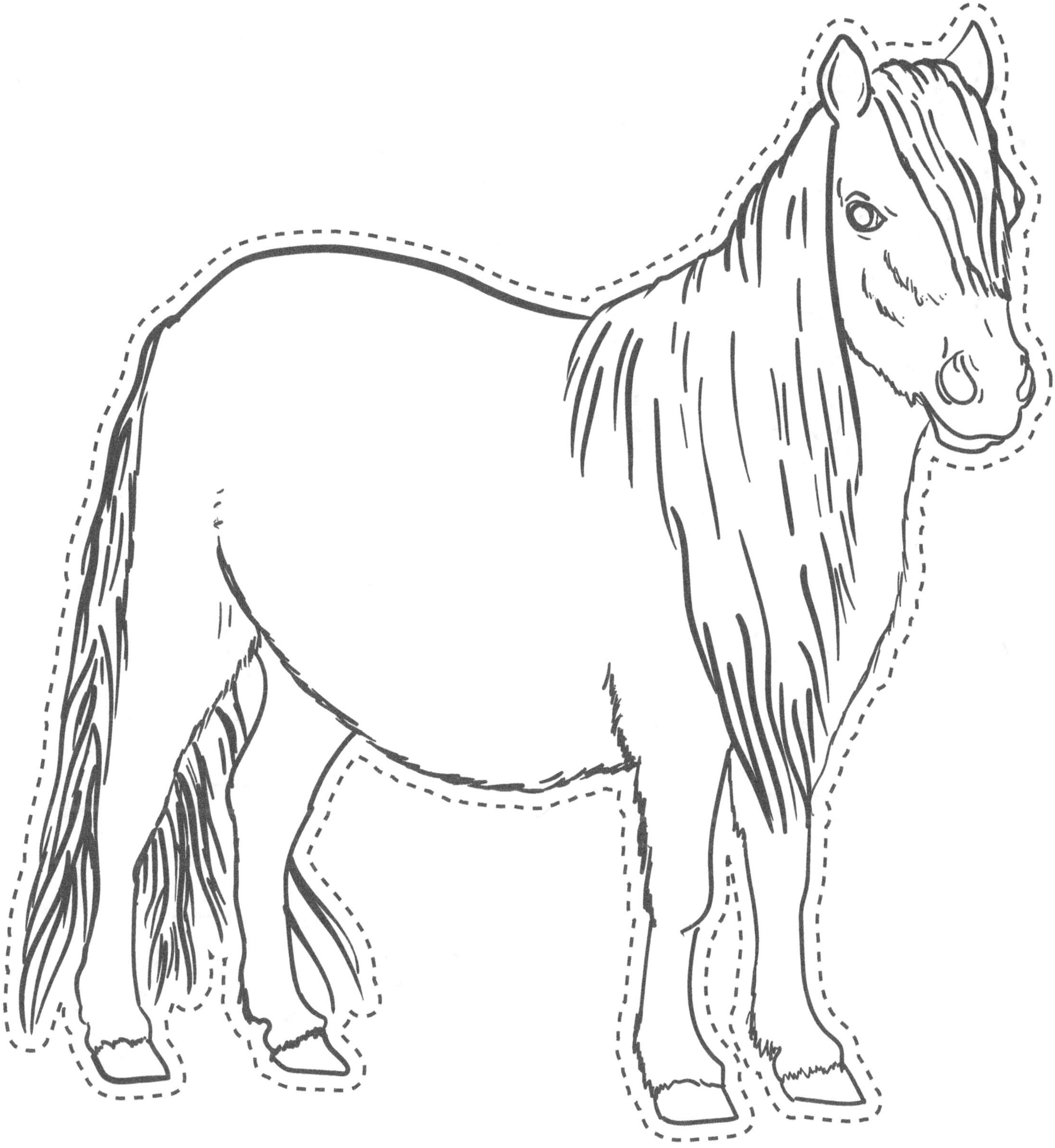

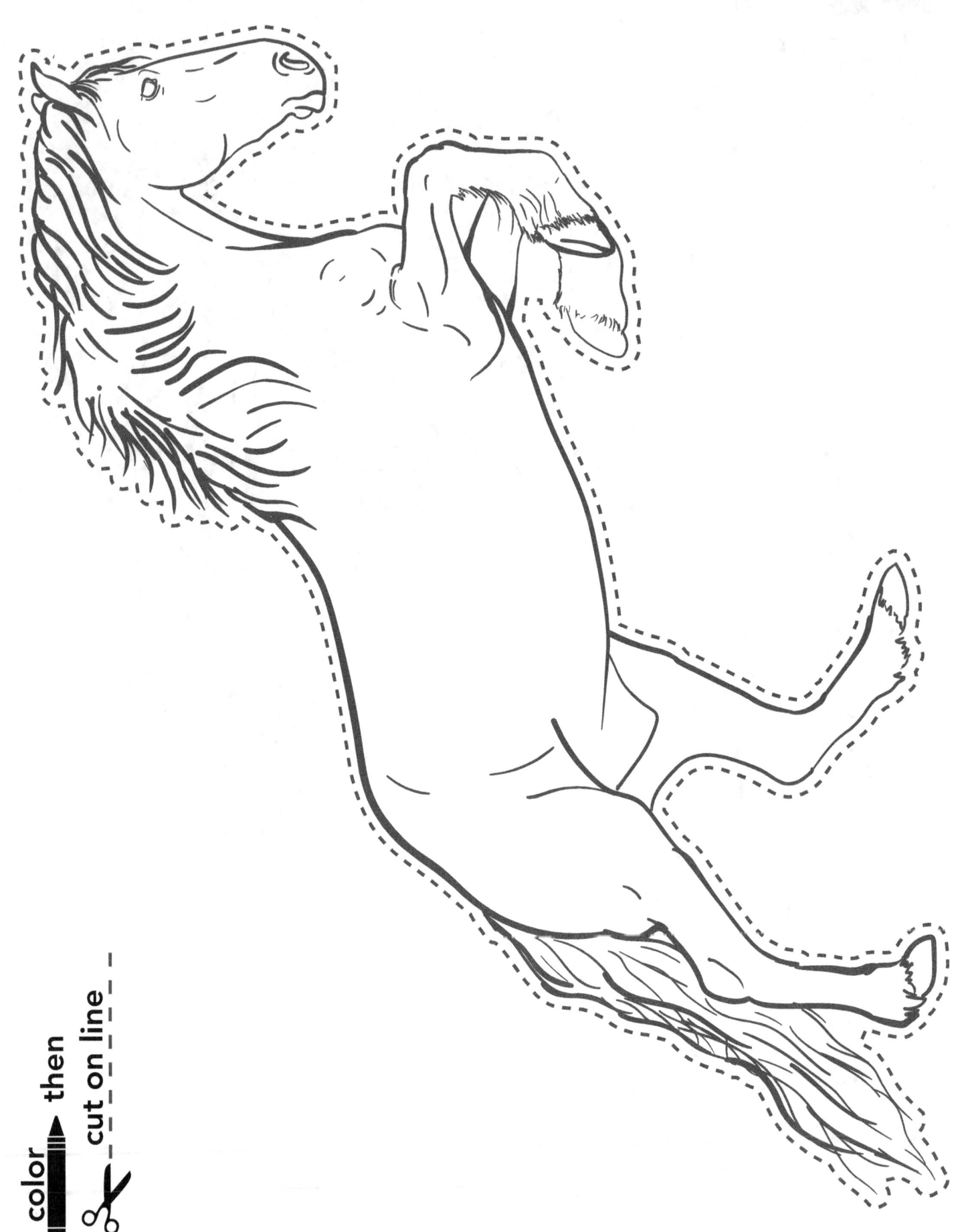

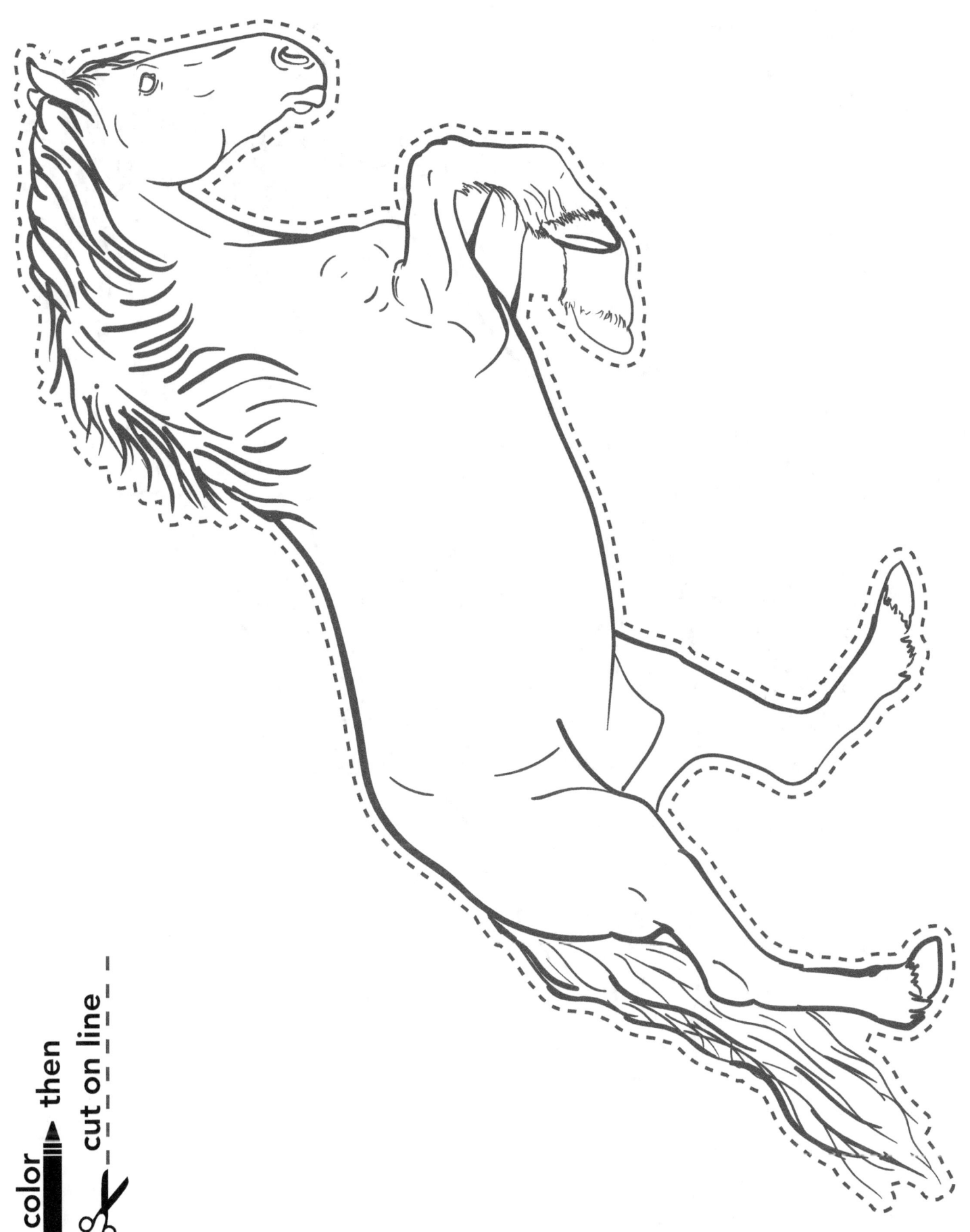

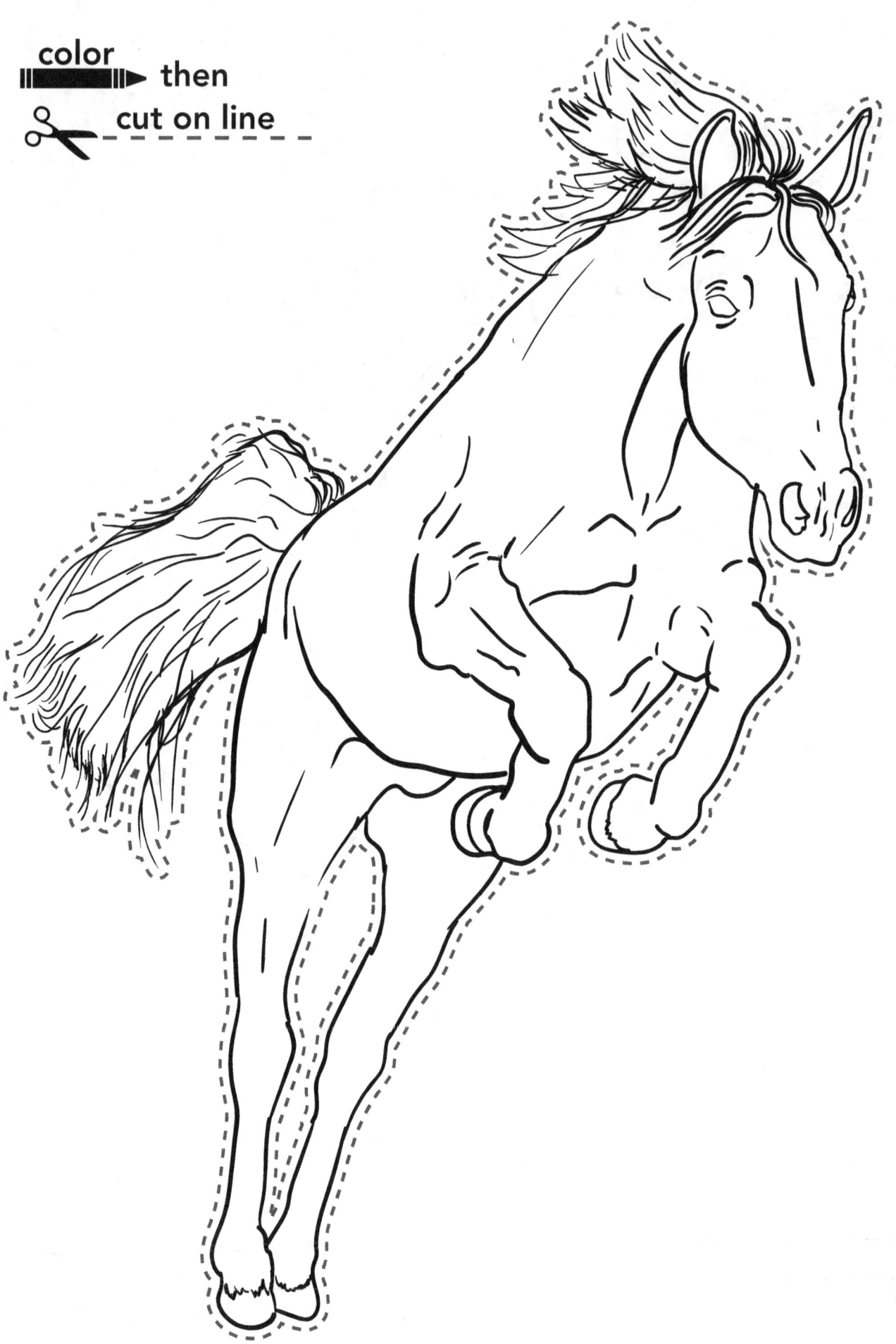

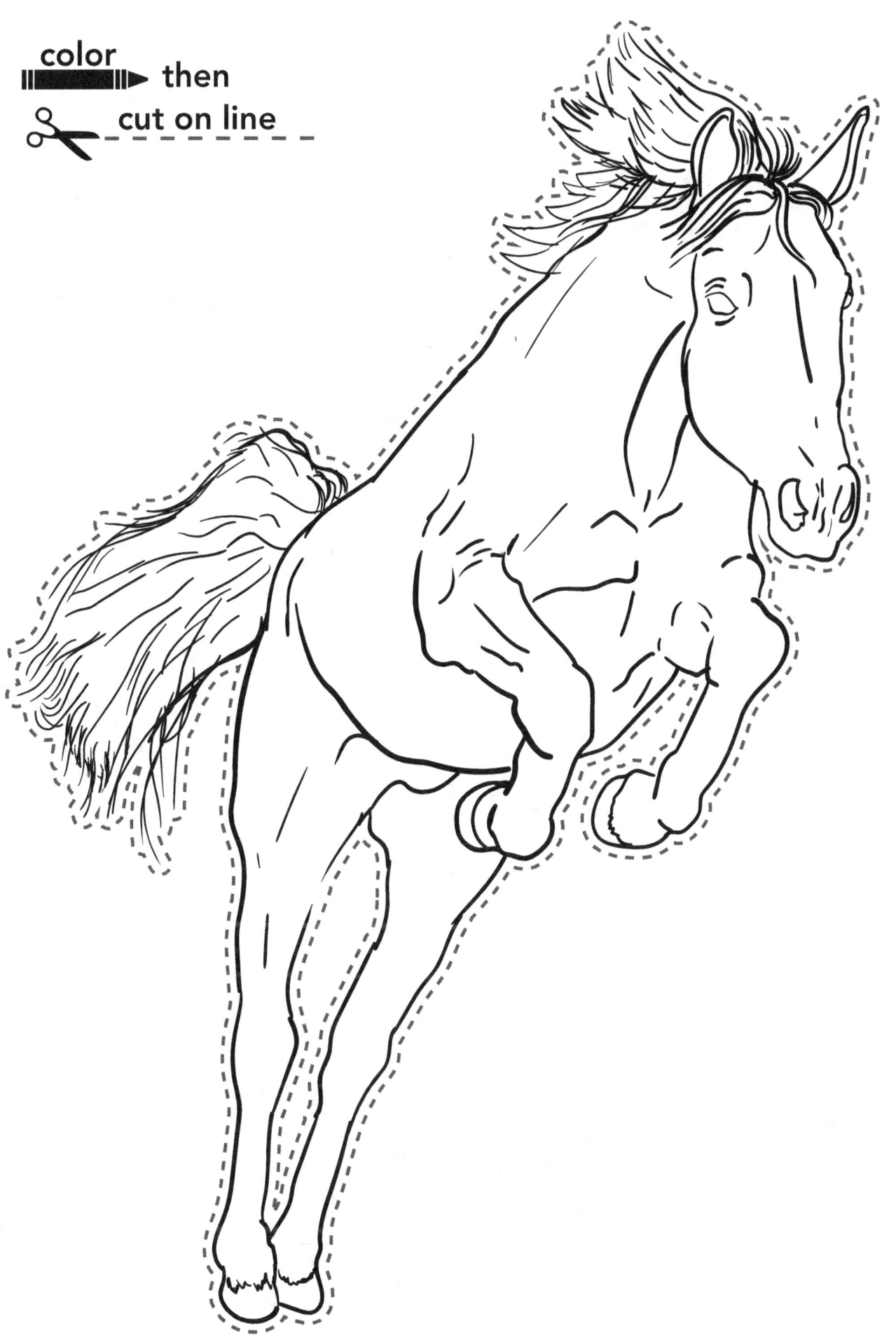

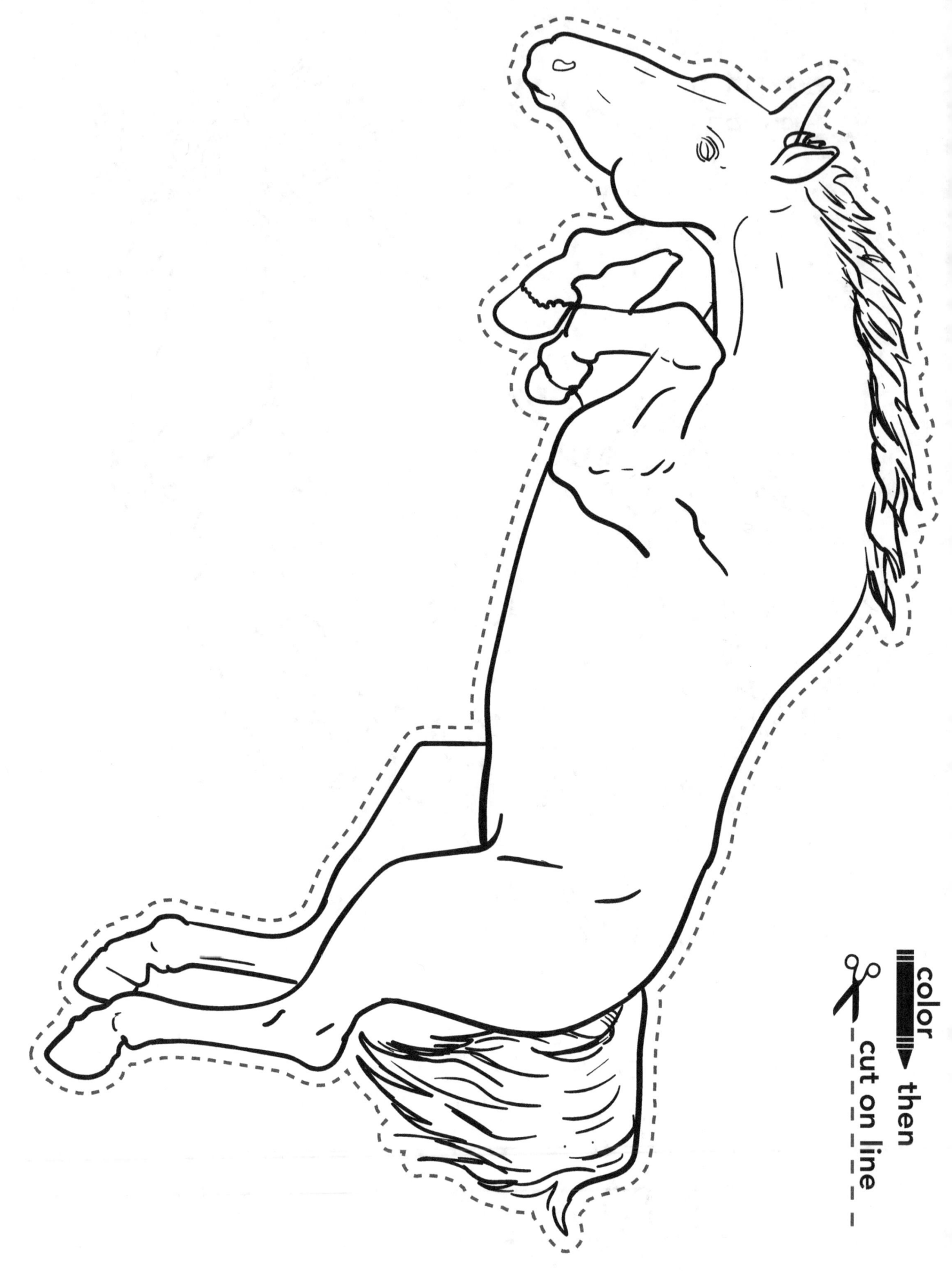

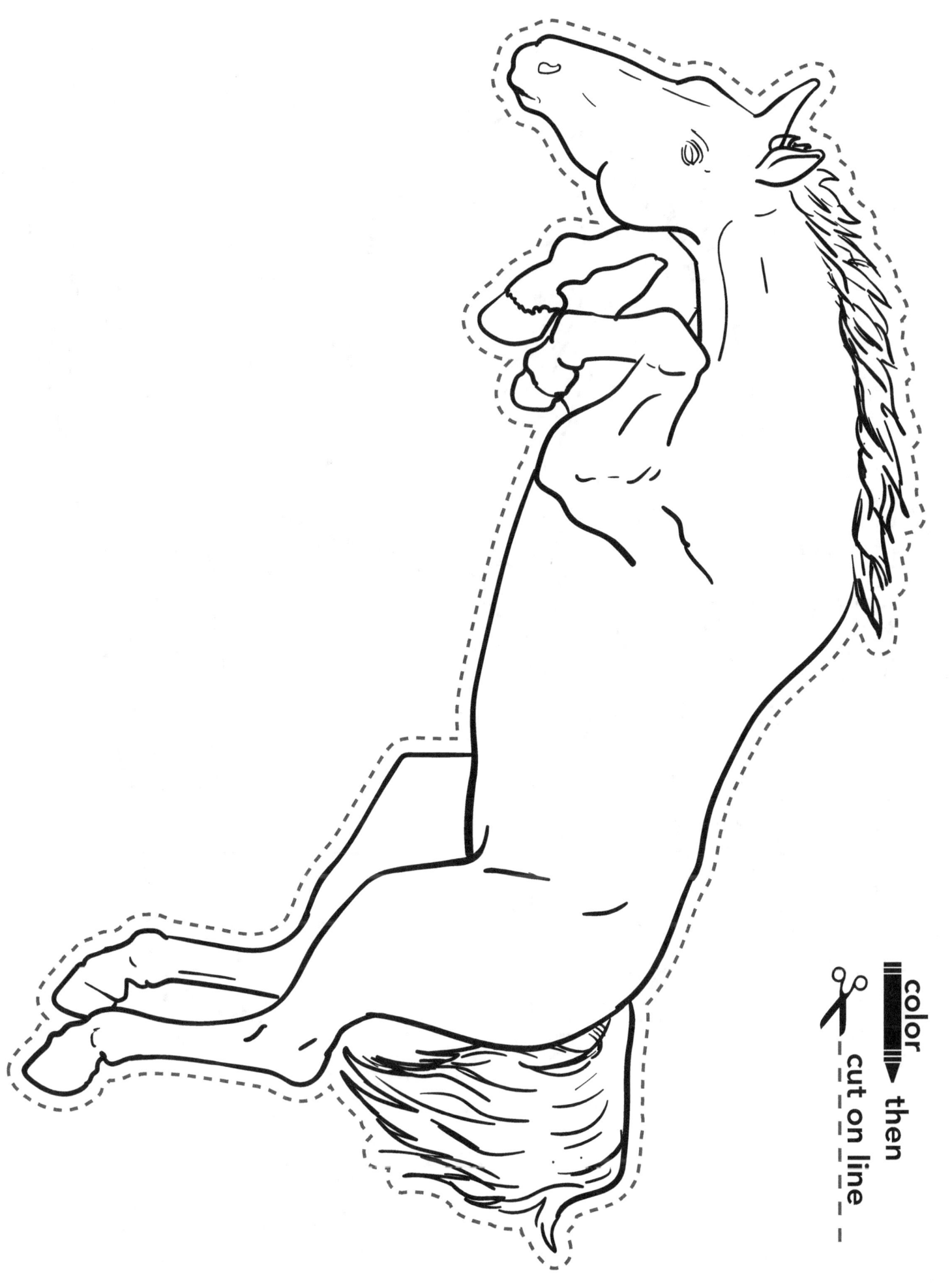

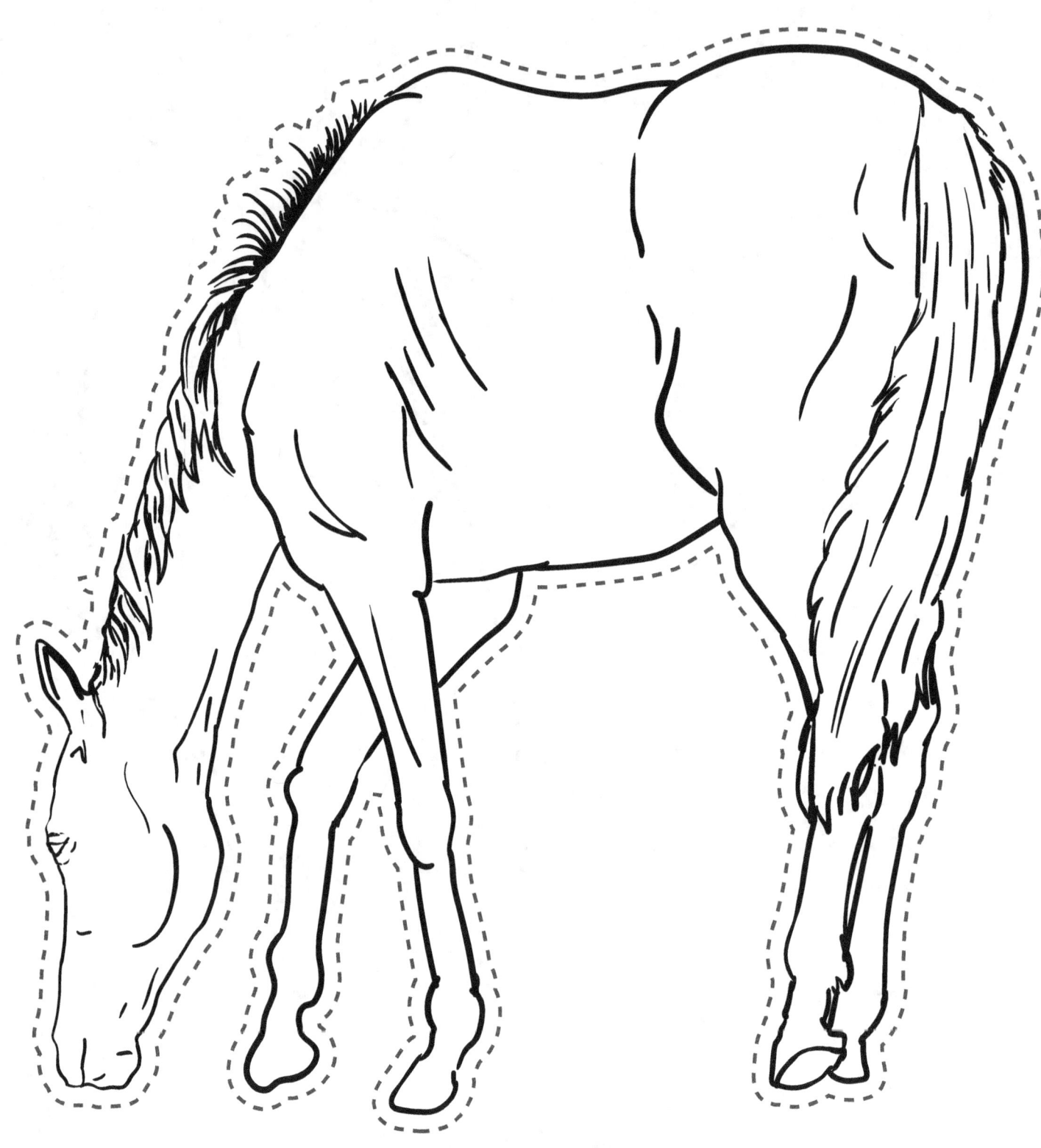

color then cut on line

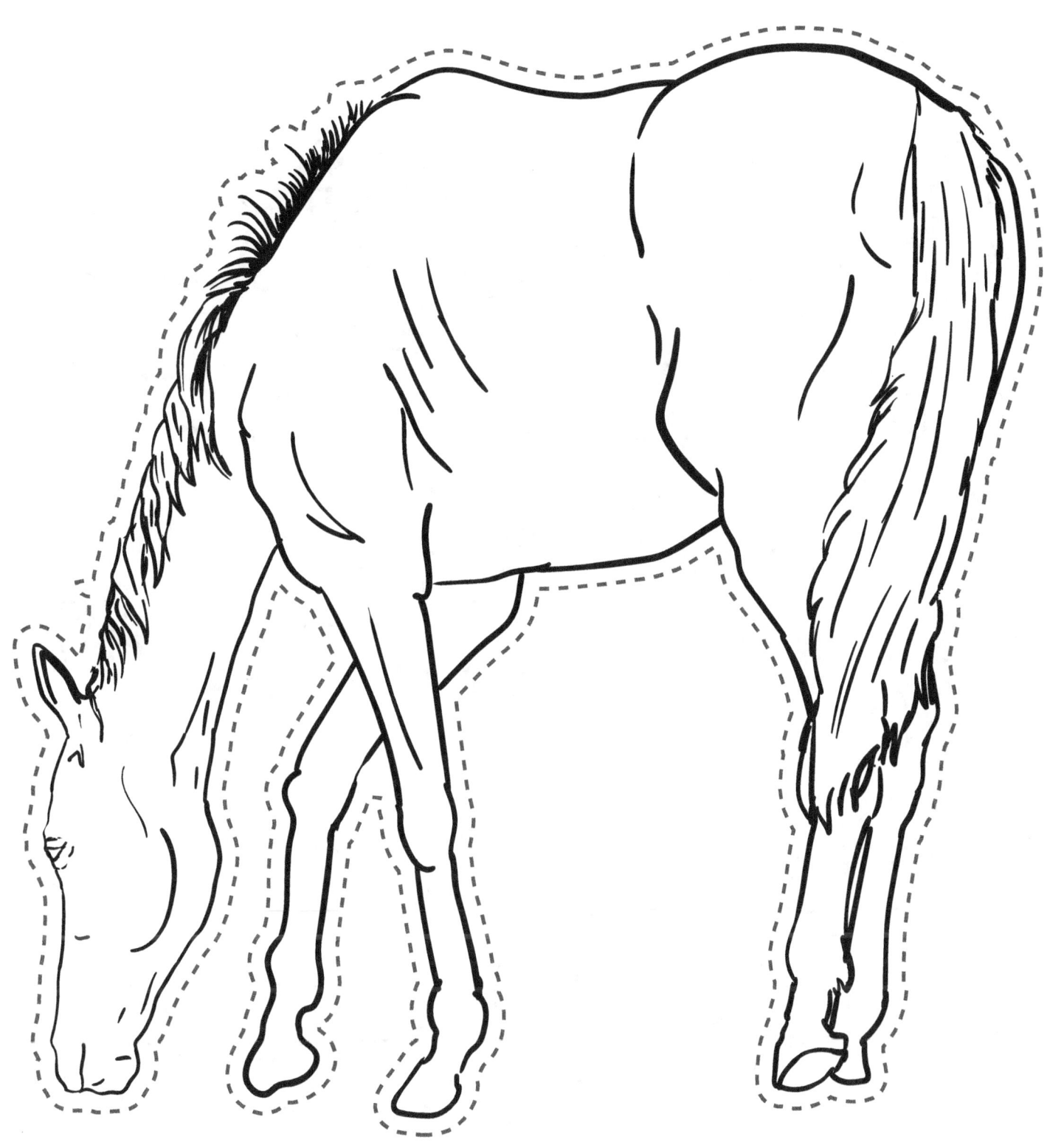

color then cut on line

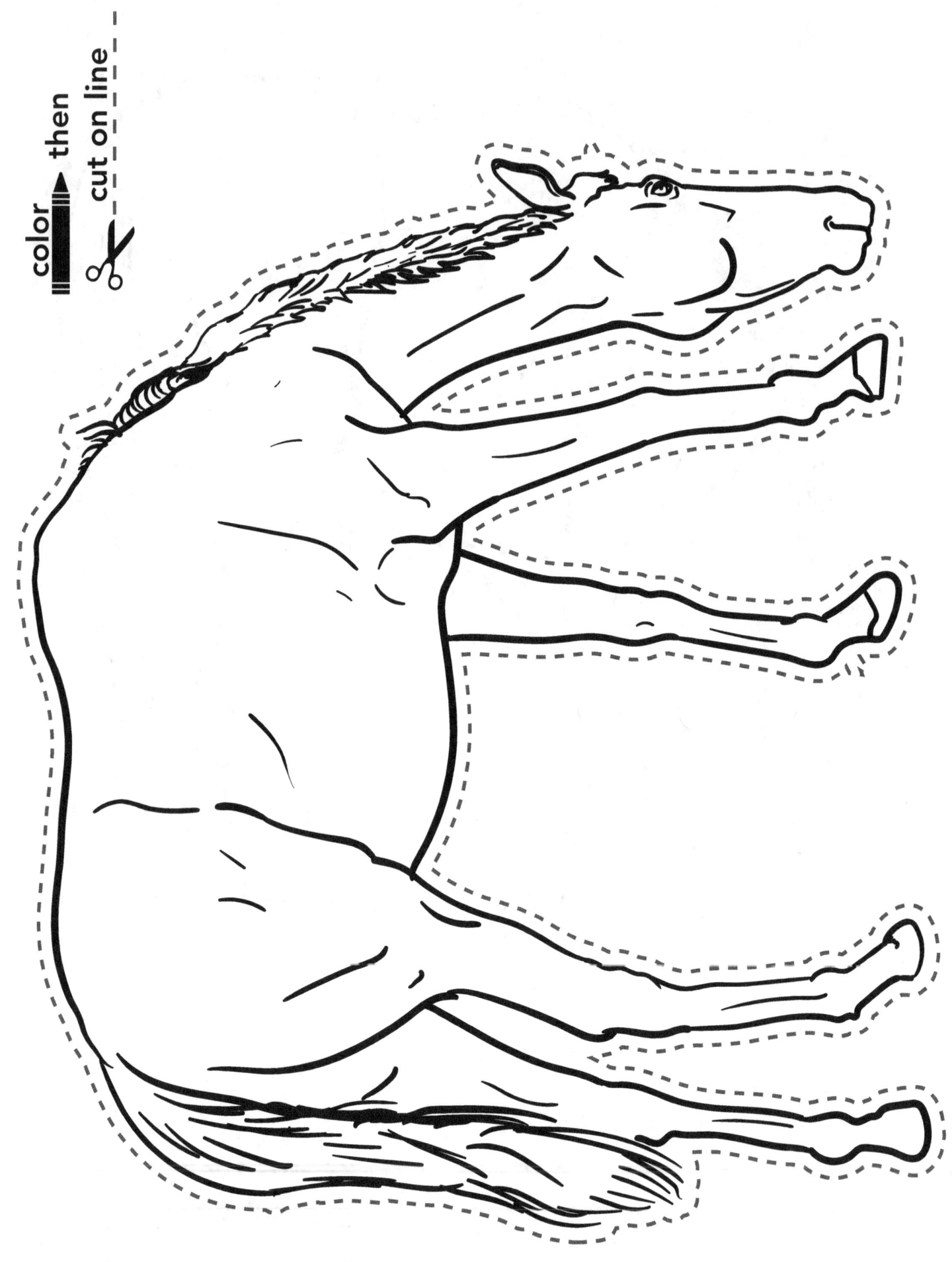

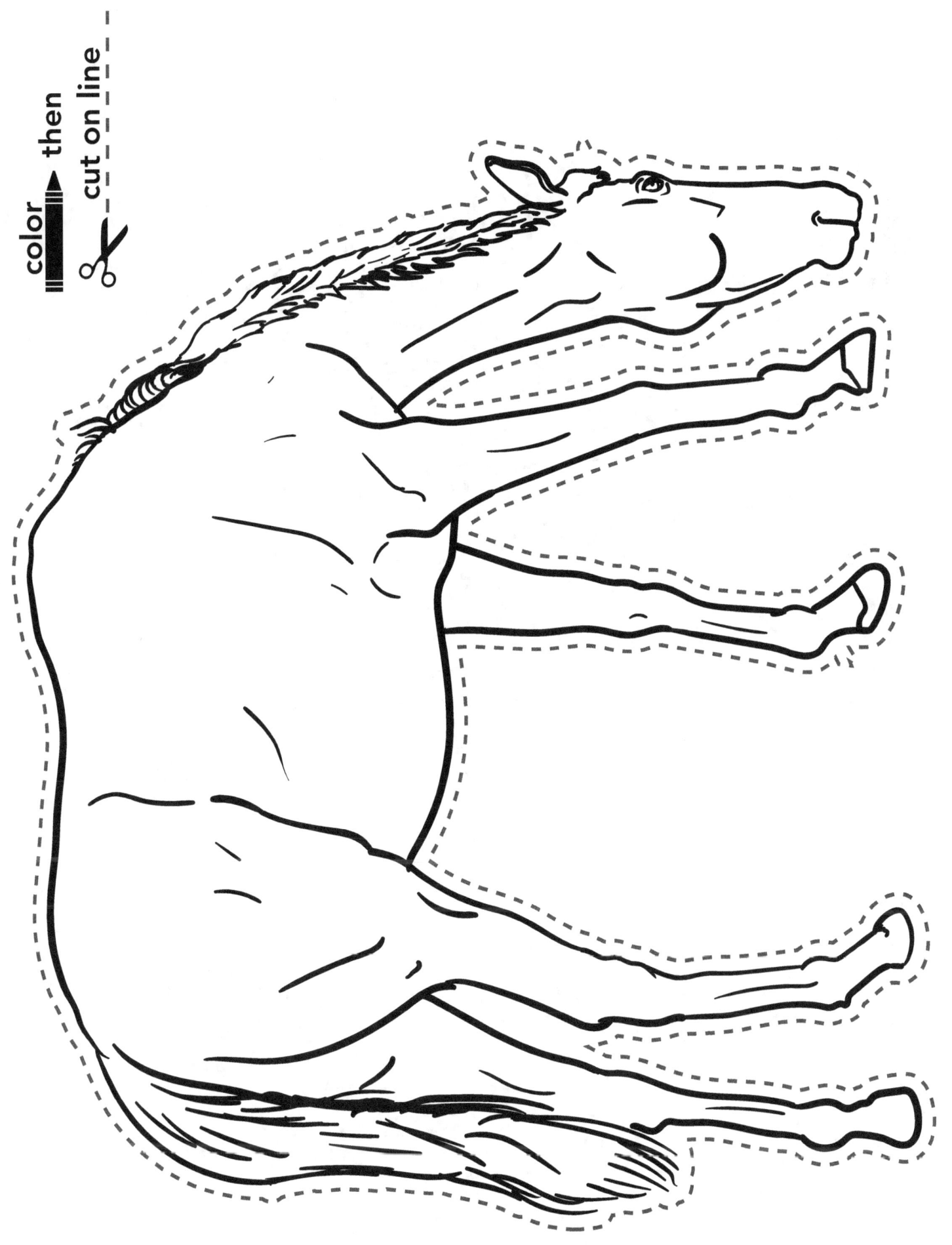

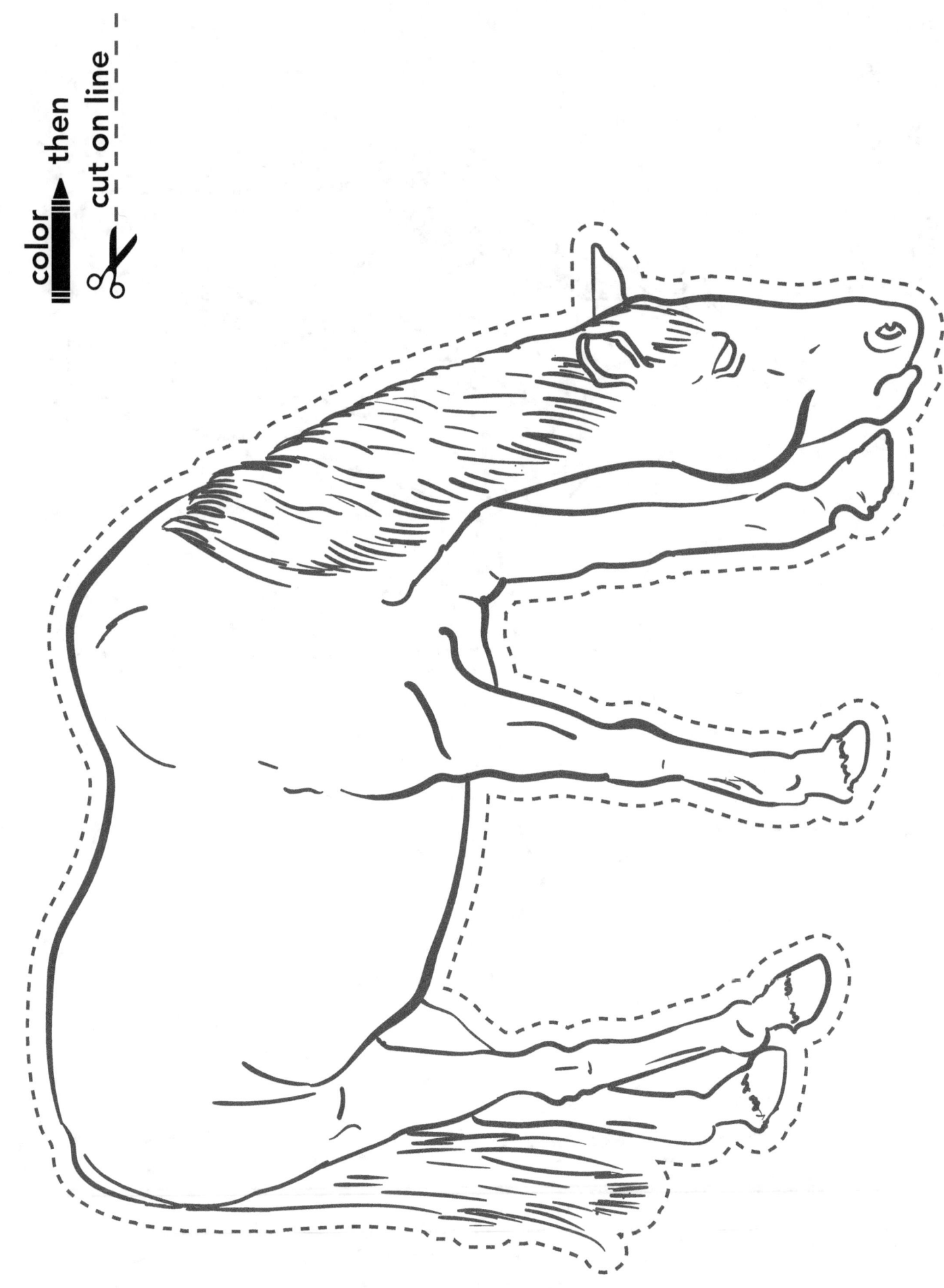

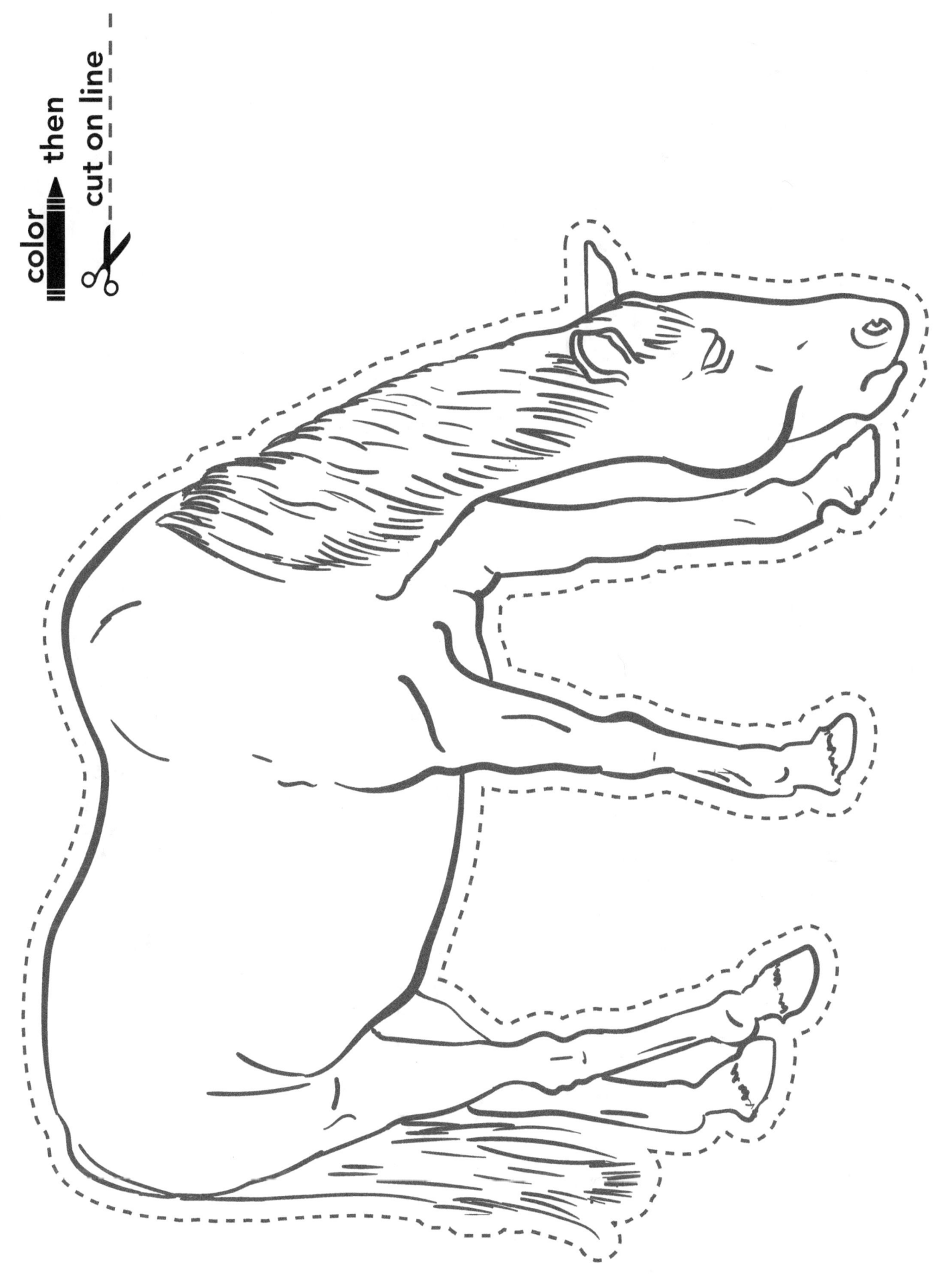

color → then
✂ cut on line

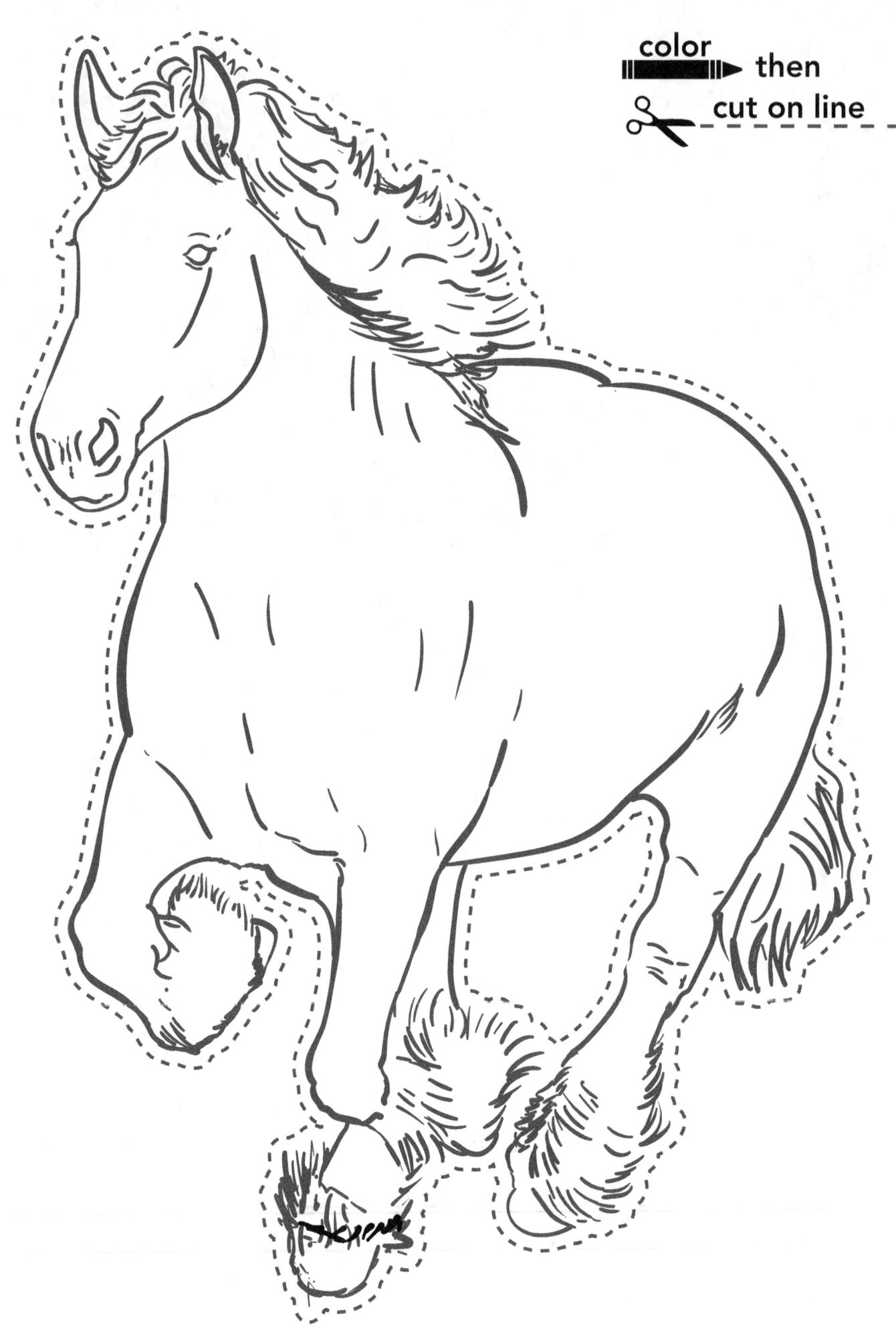

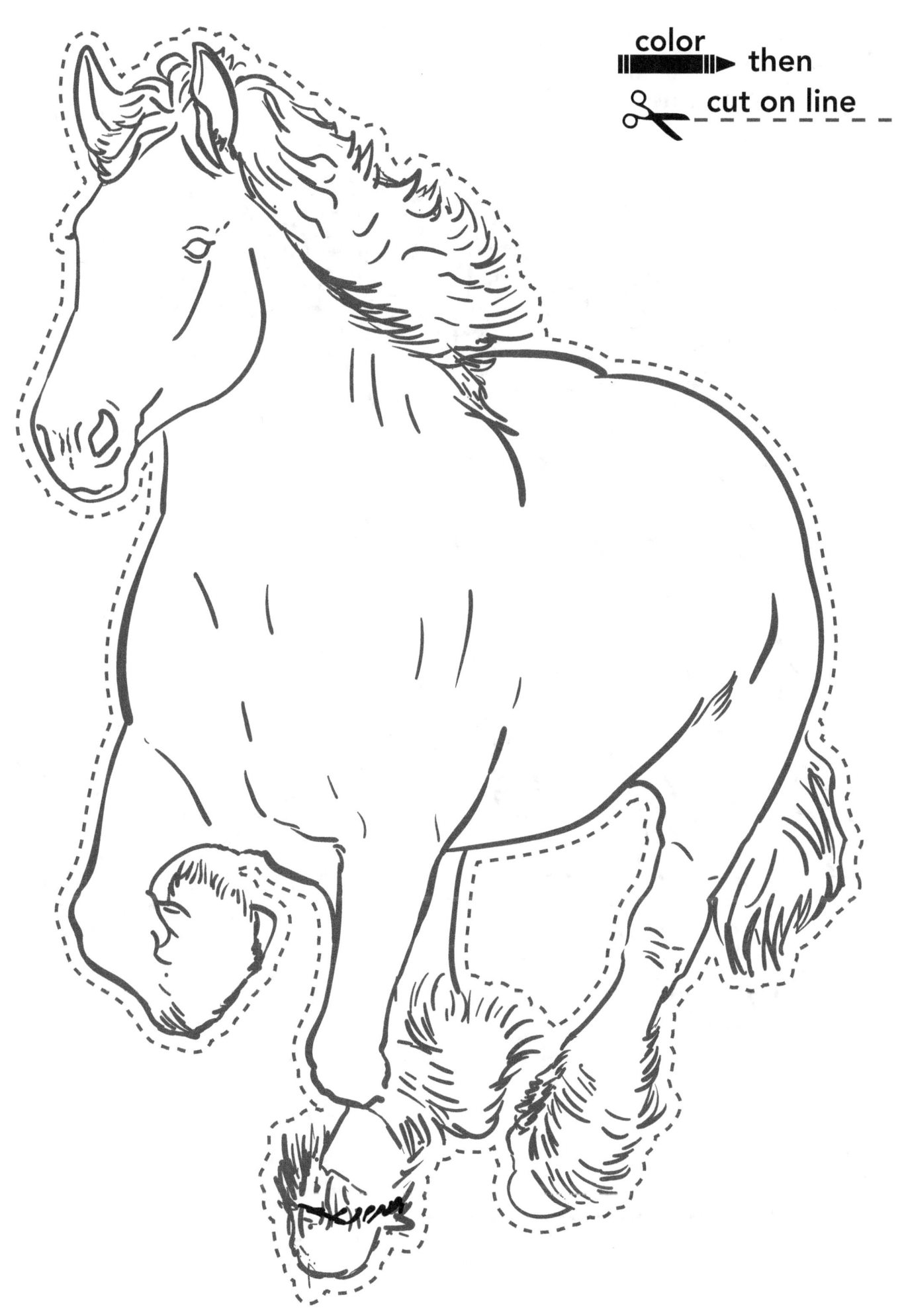

color then cut on line

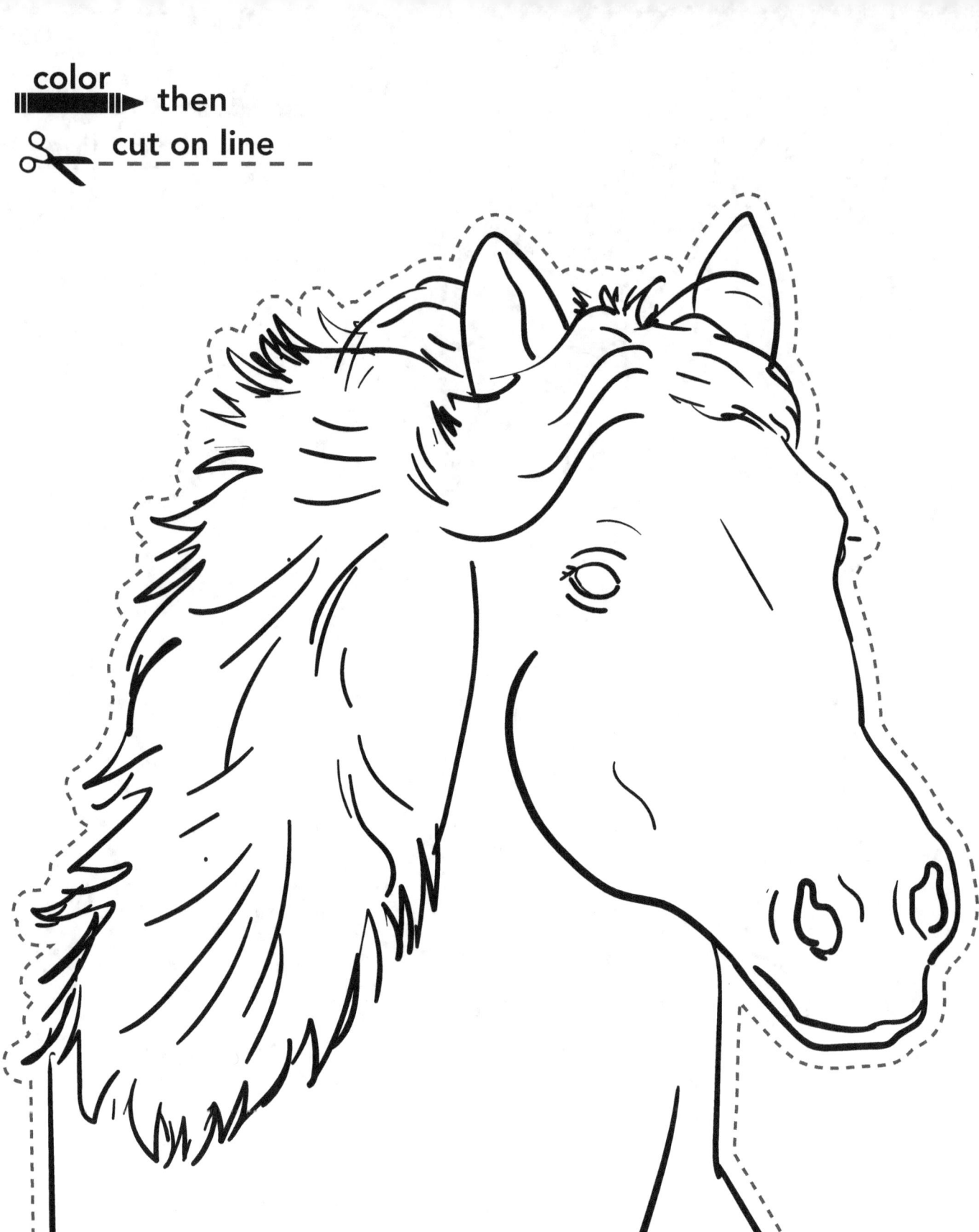

color then cut on line

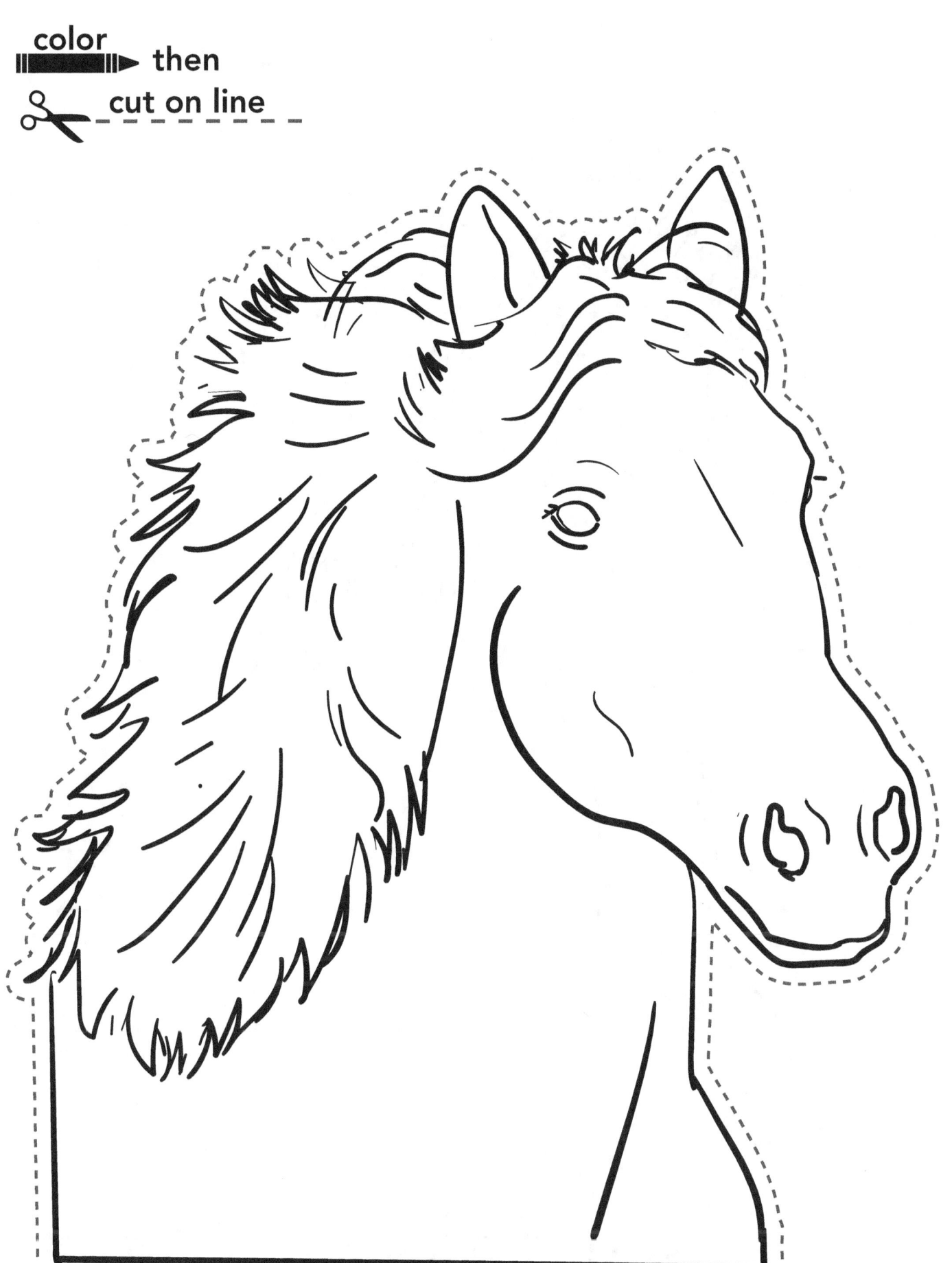

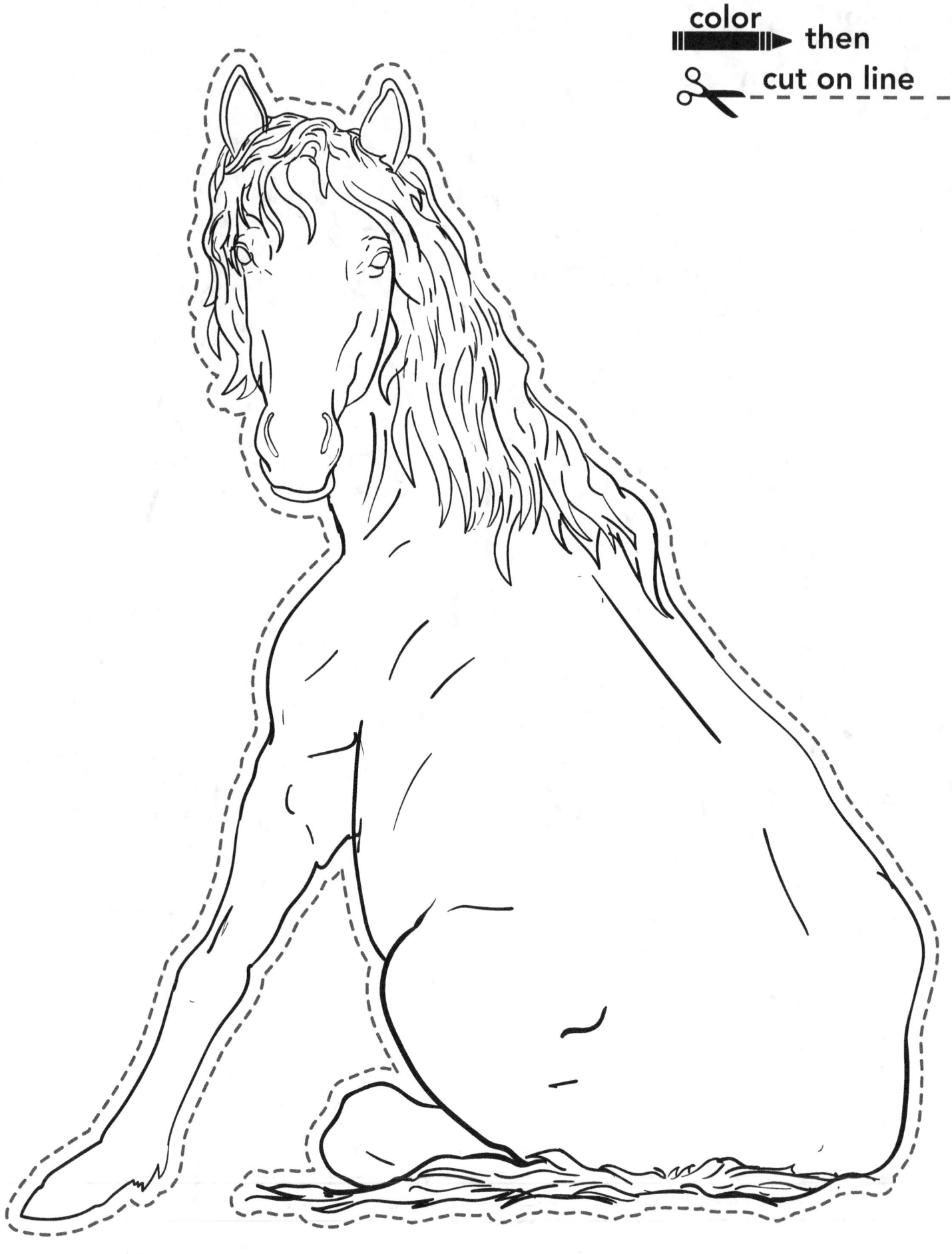

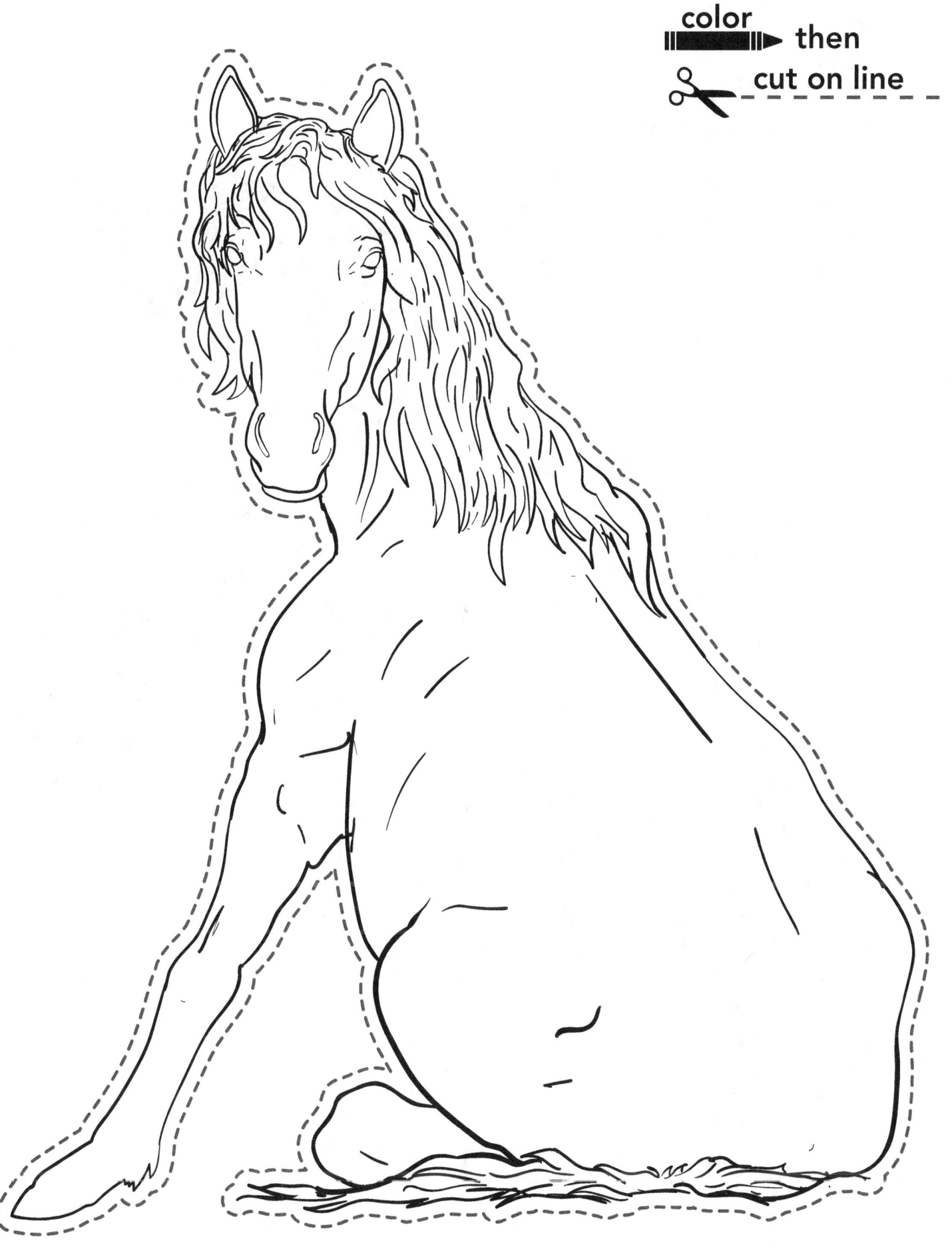

color then cut on line

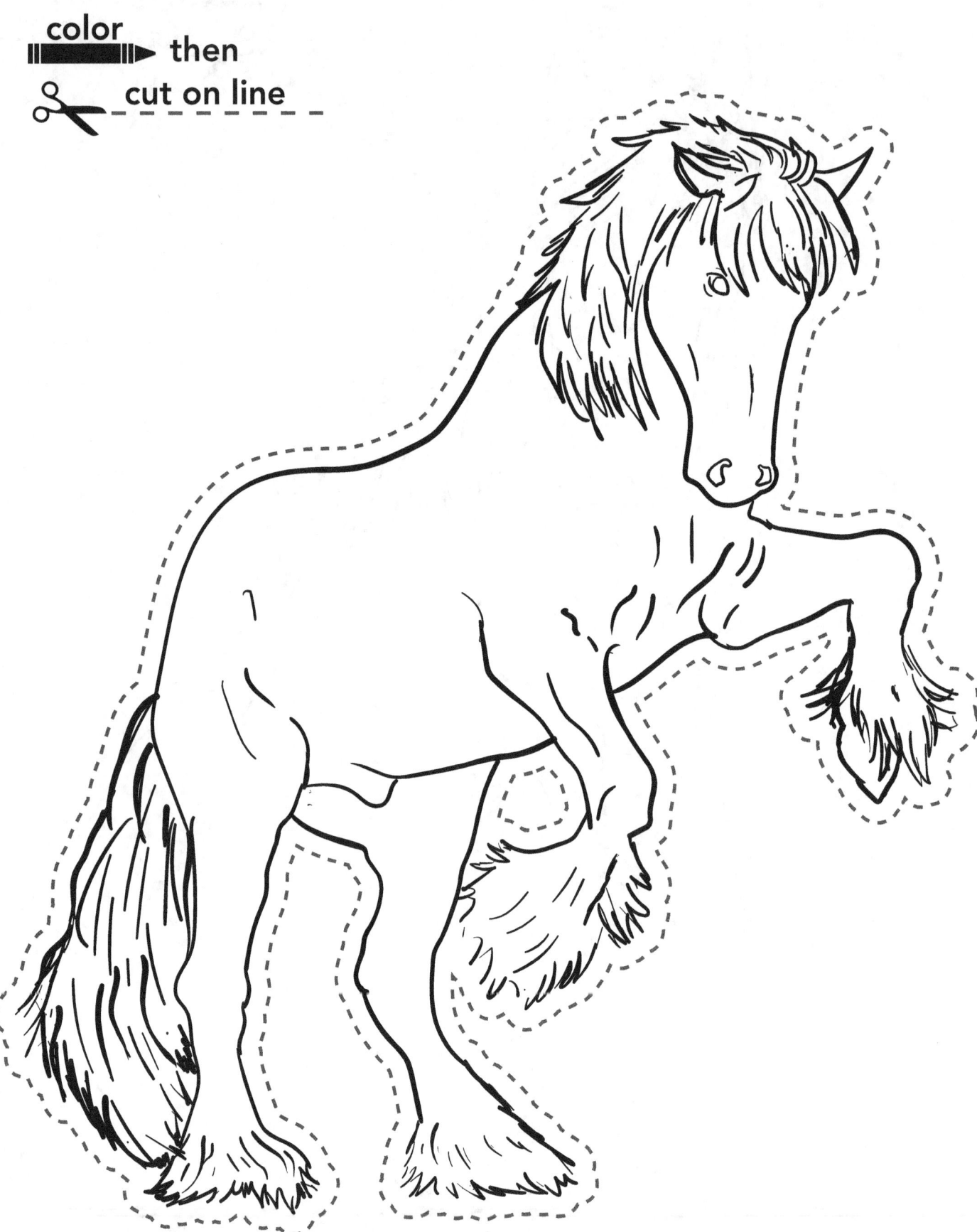

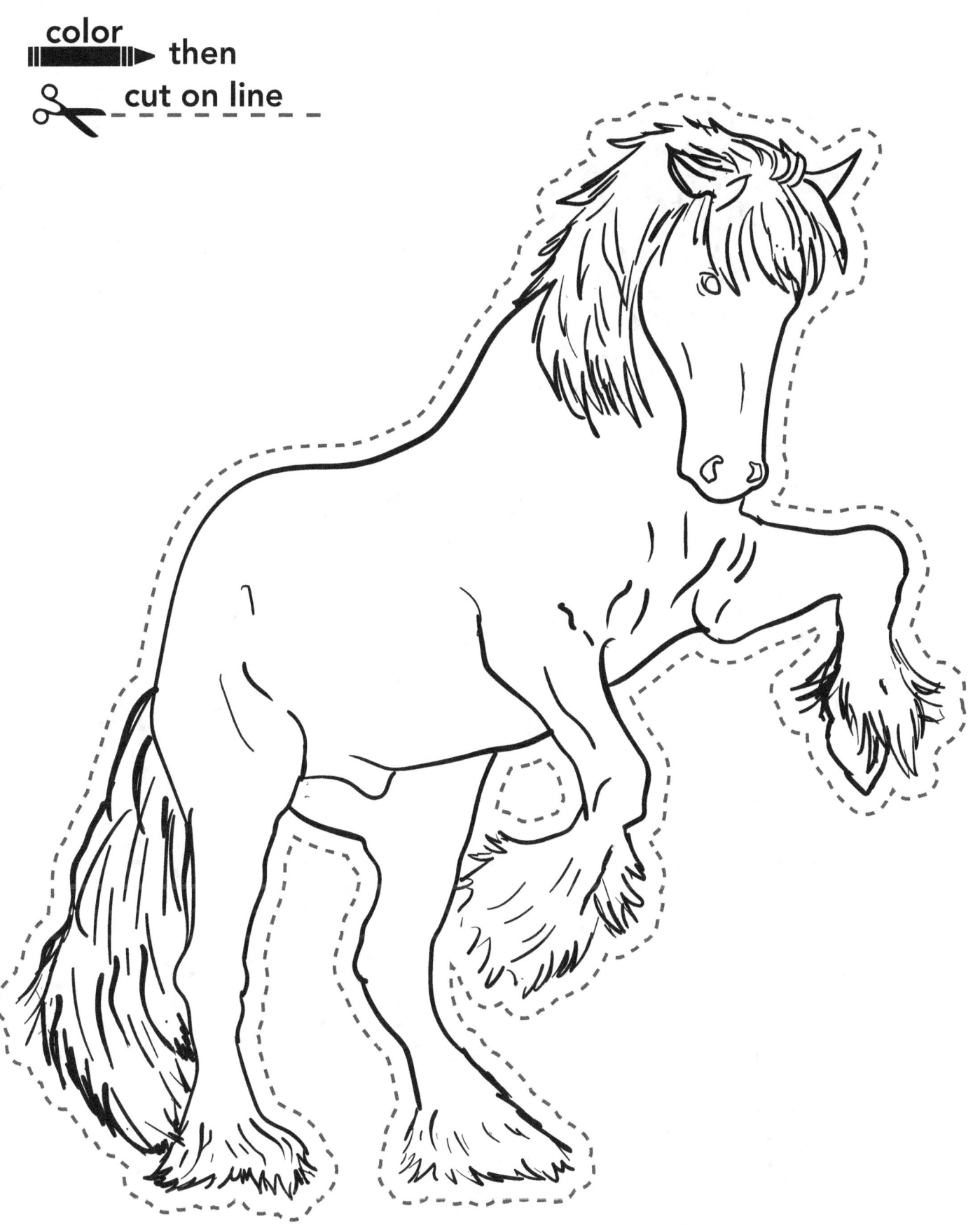

color ▶ then
✂ cut on line

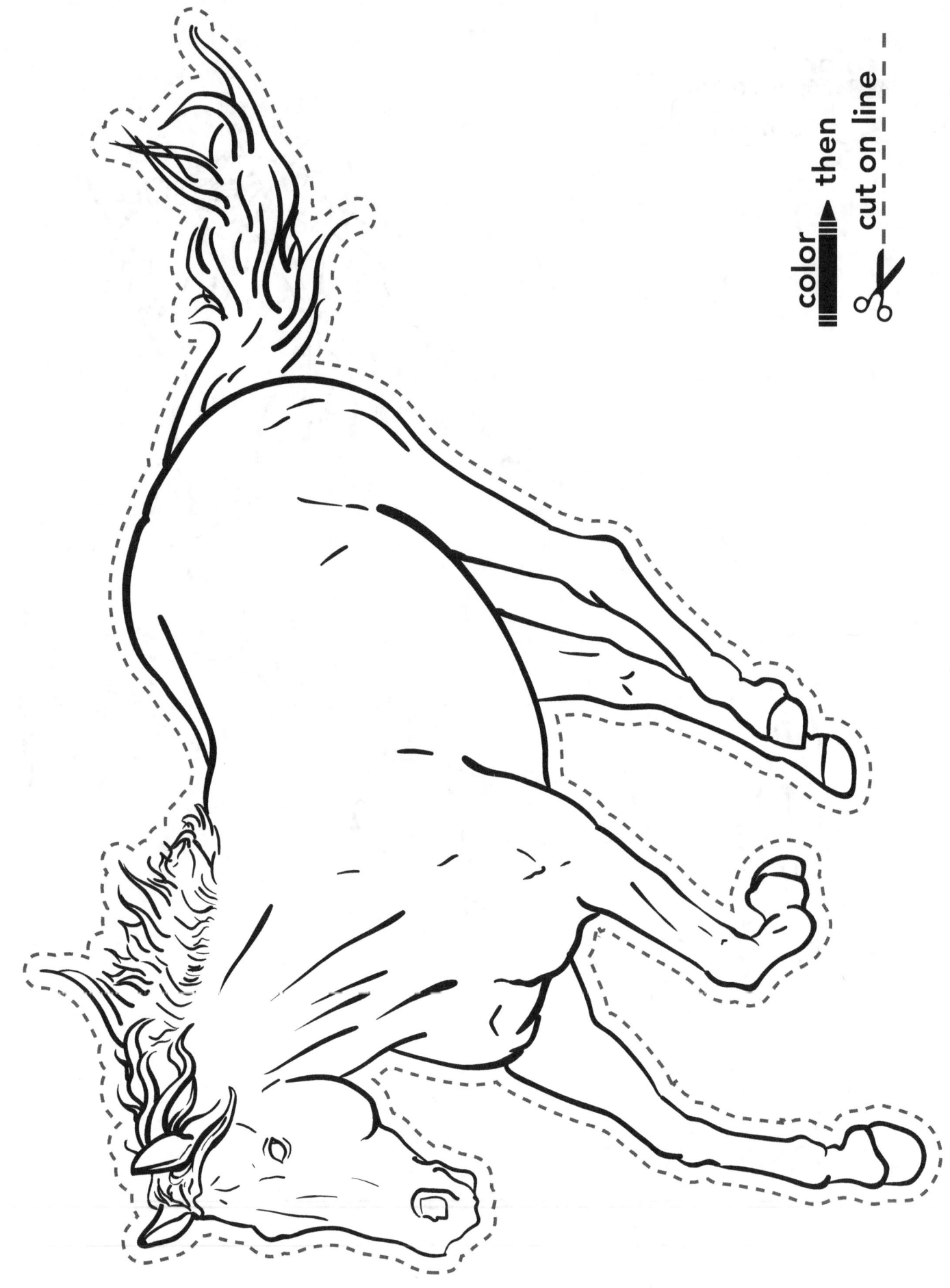

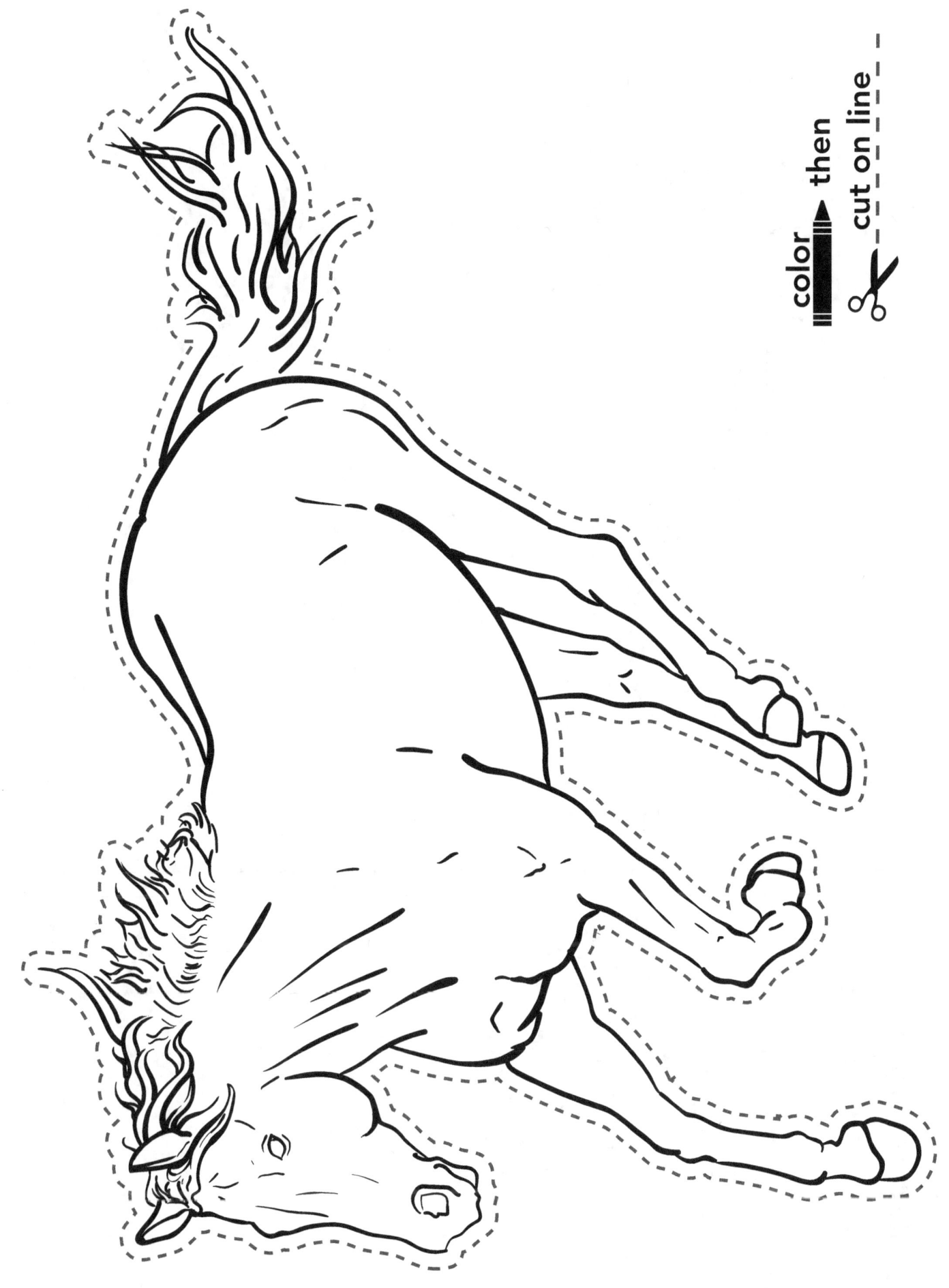

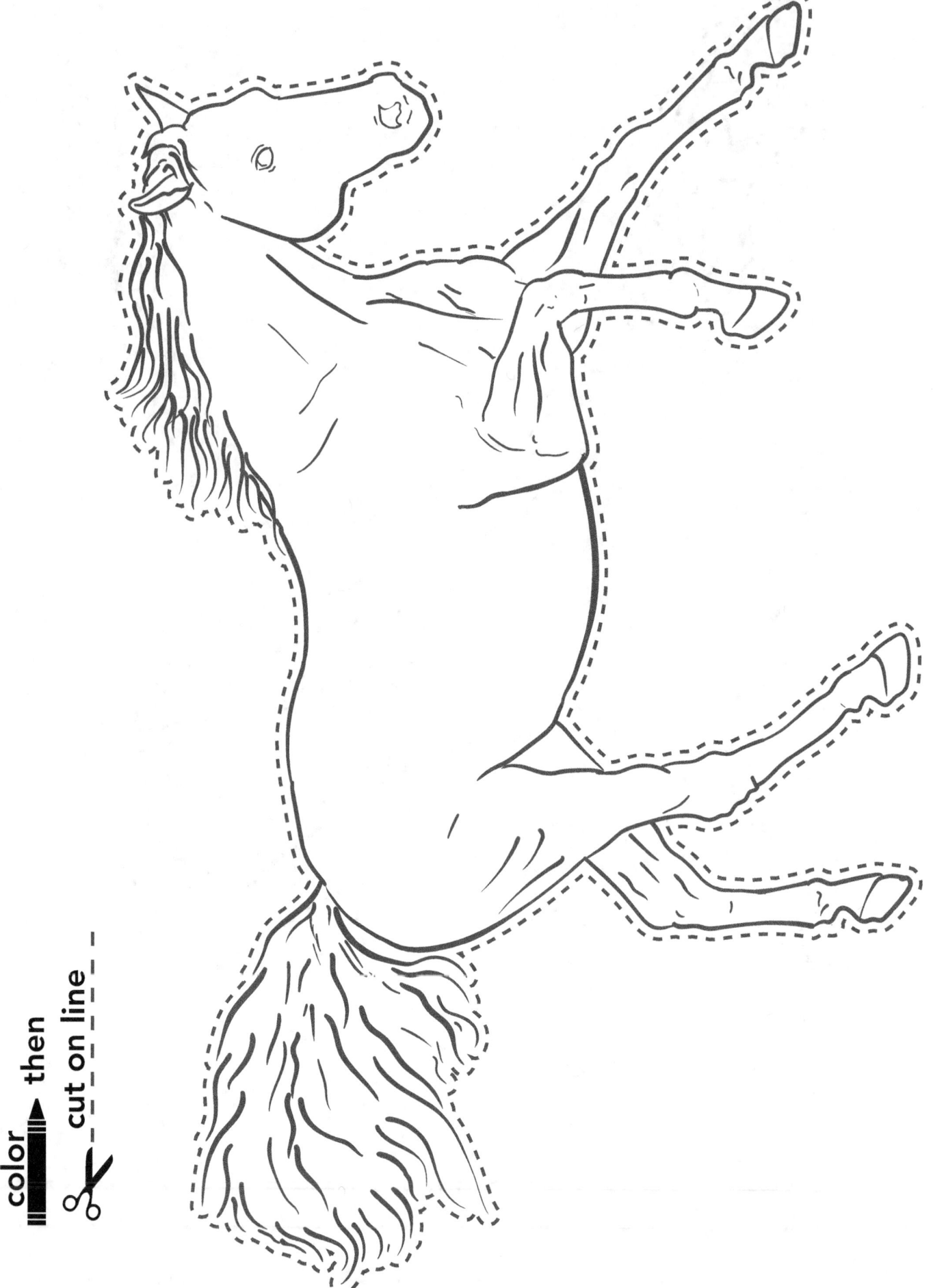

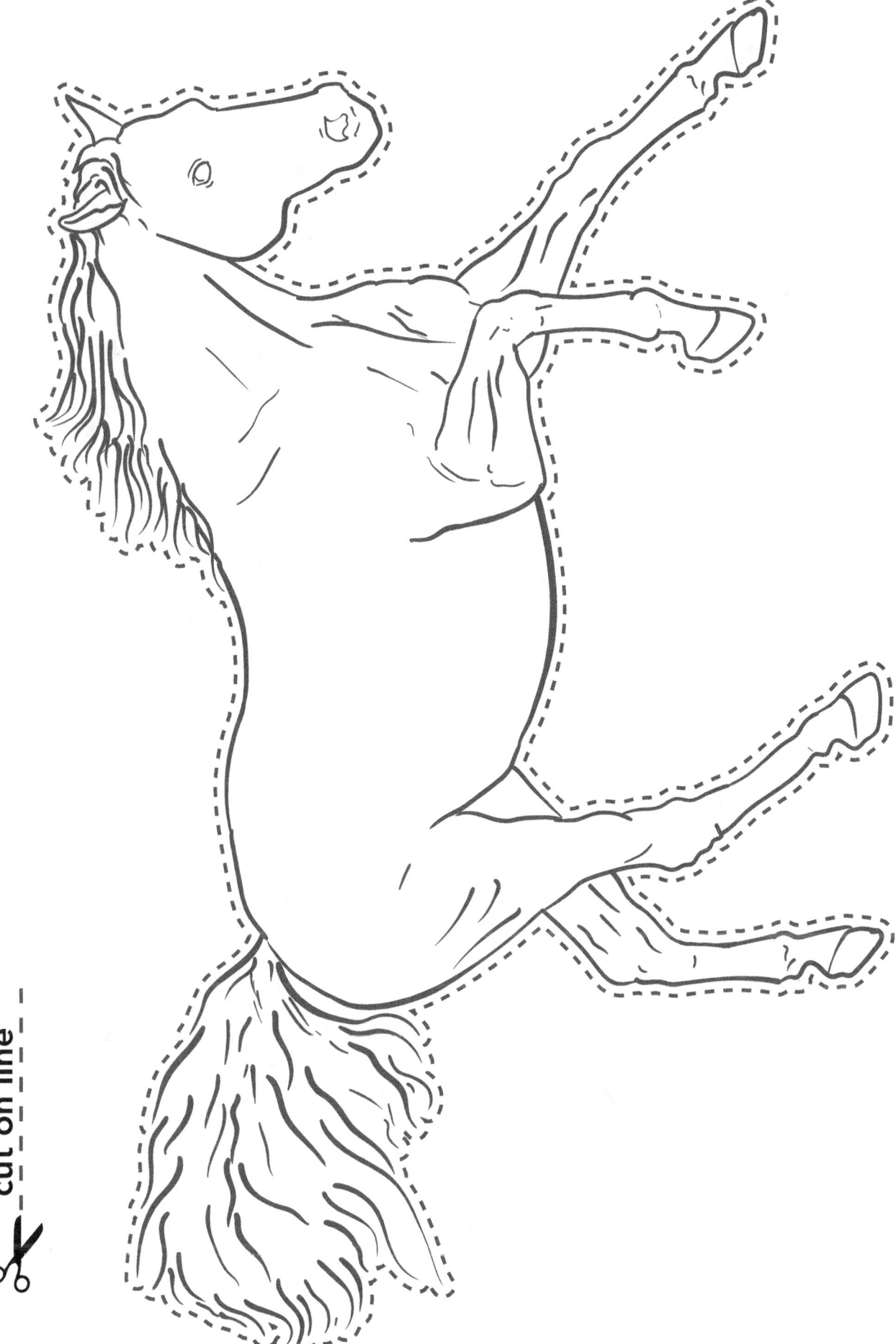

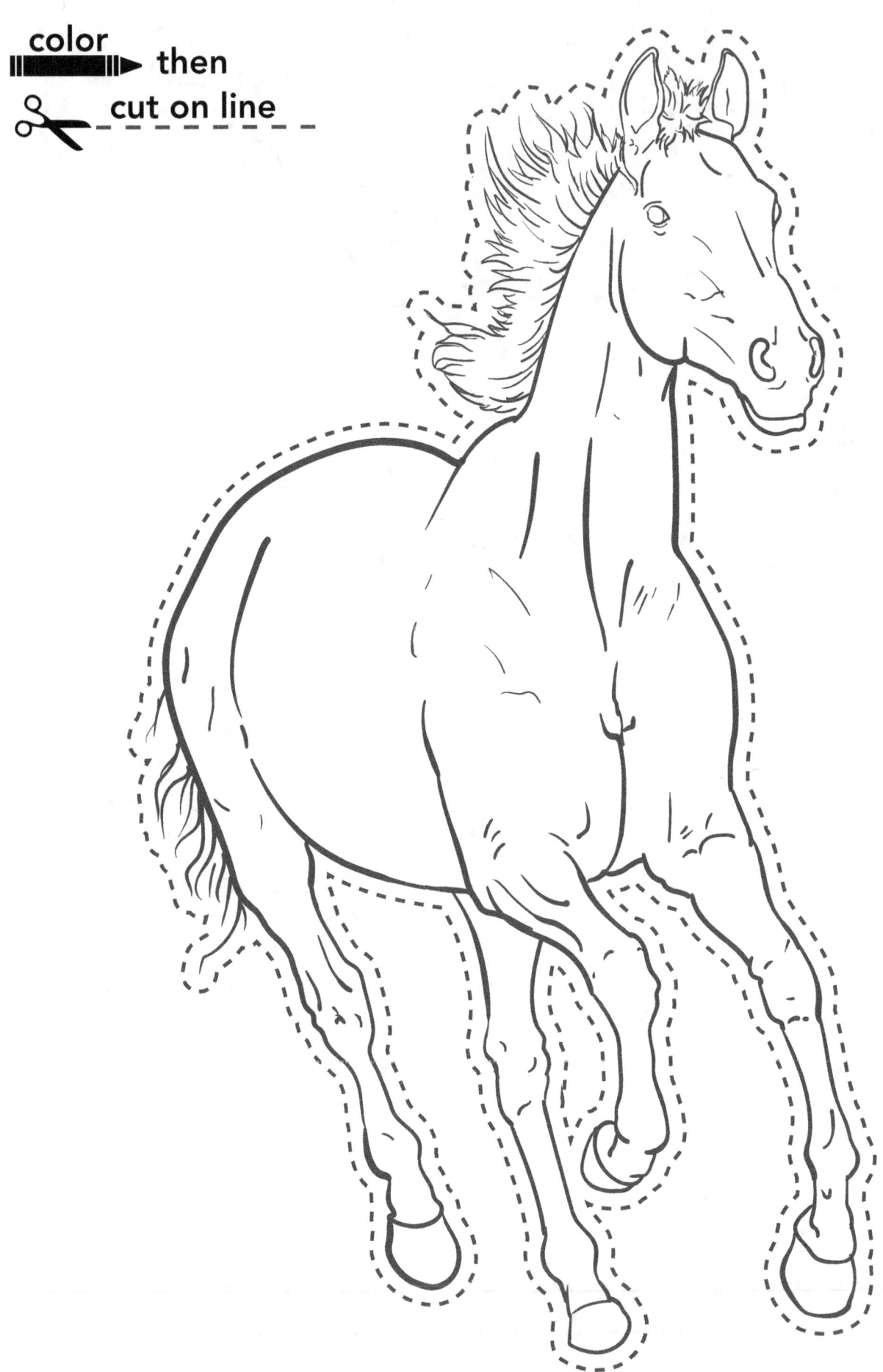

color then
cut on line

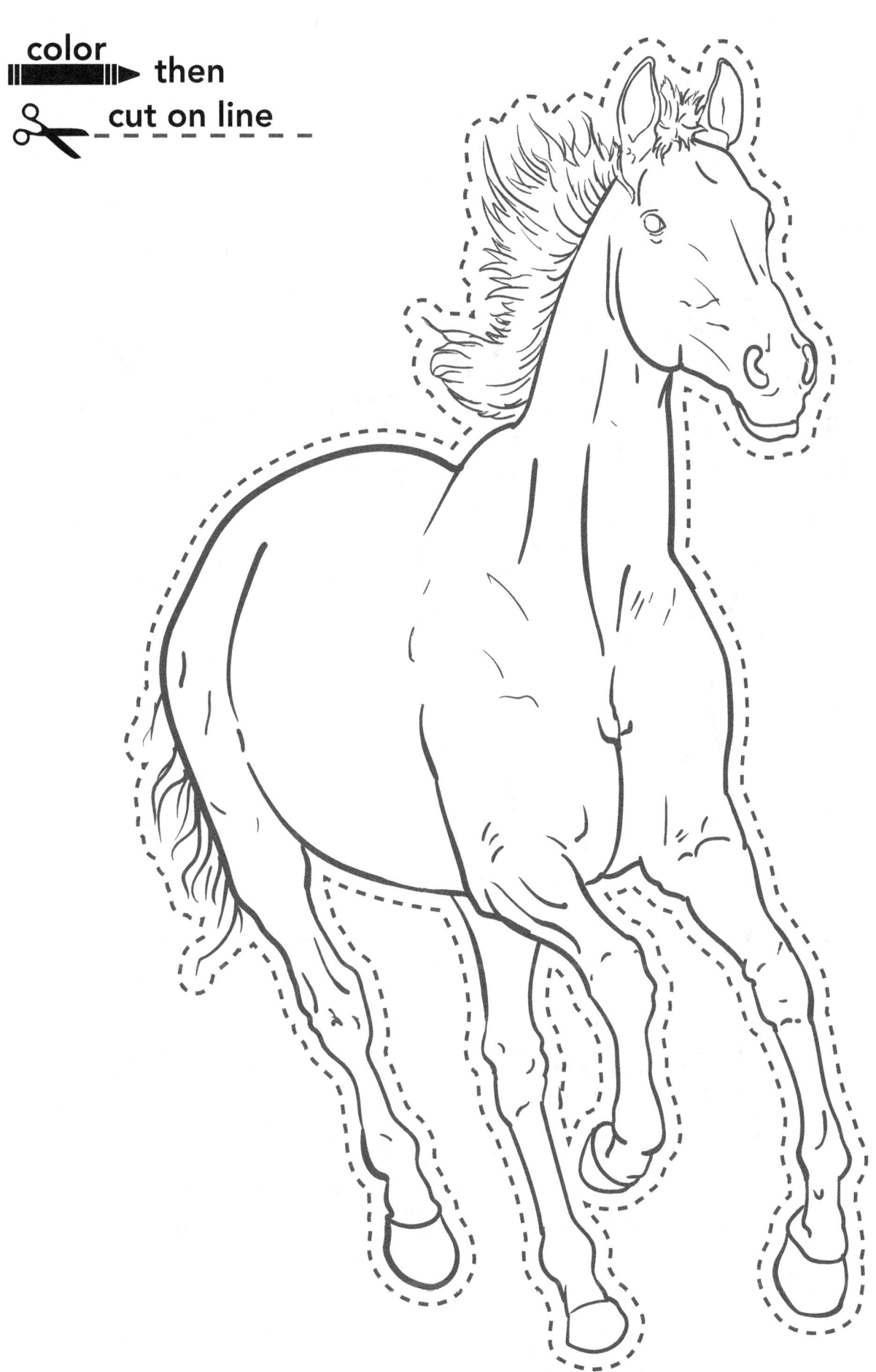

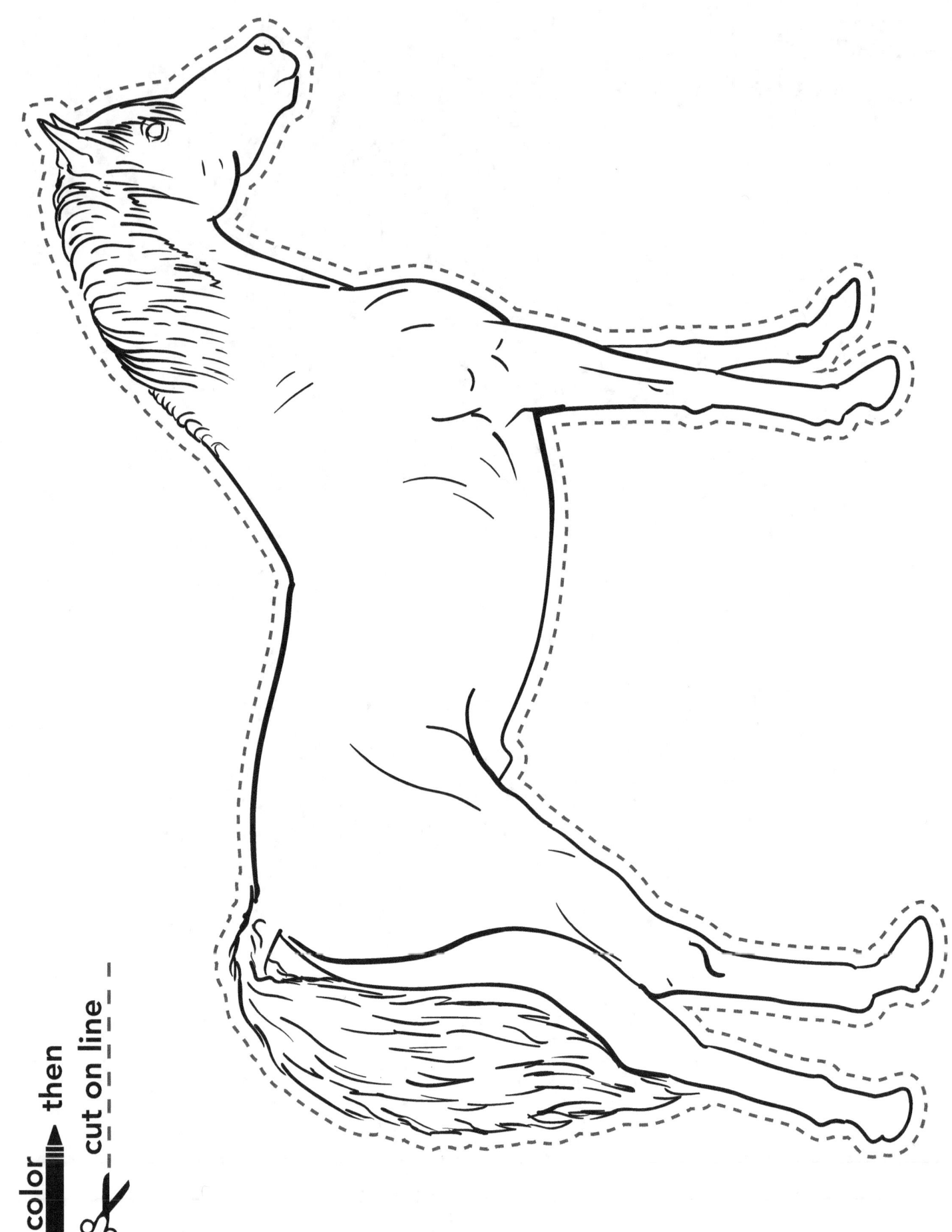

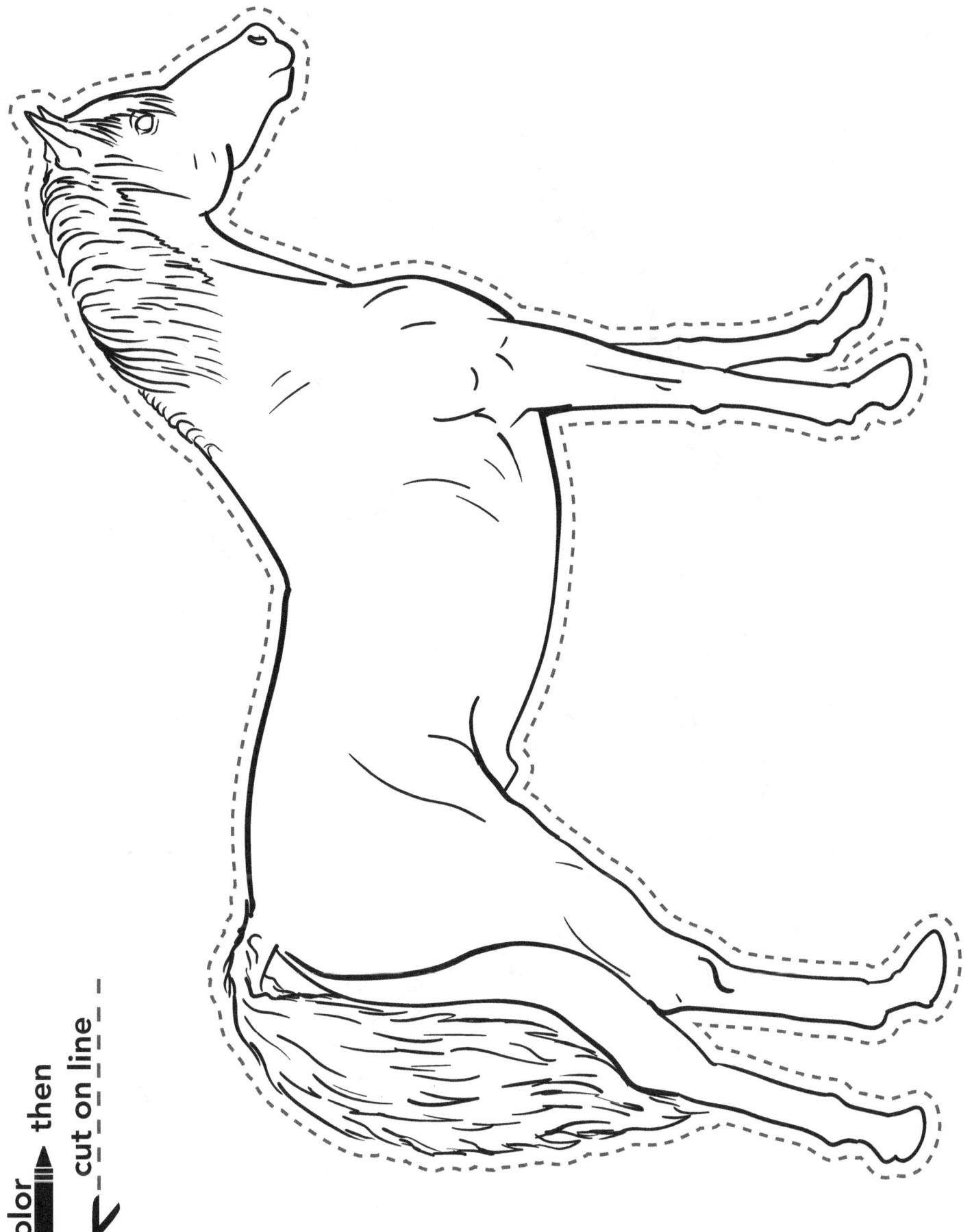

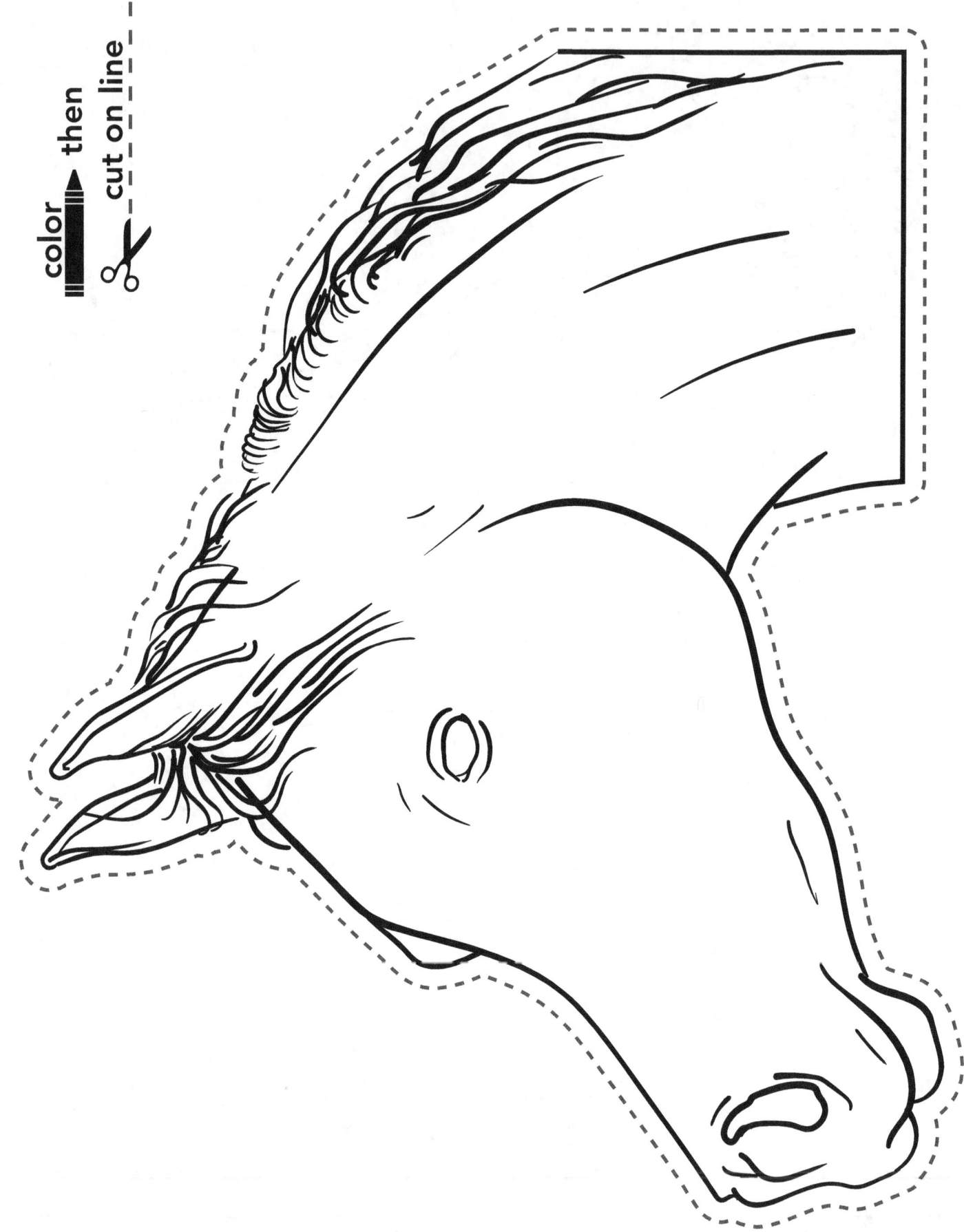

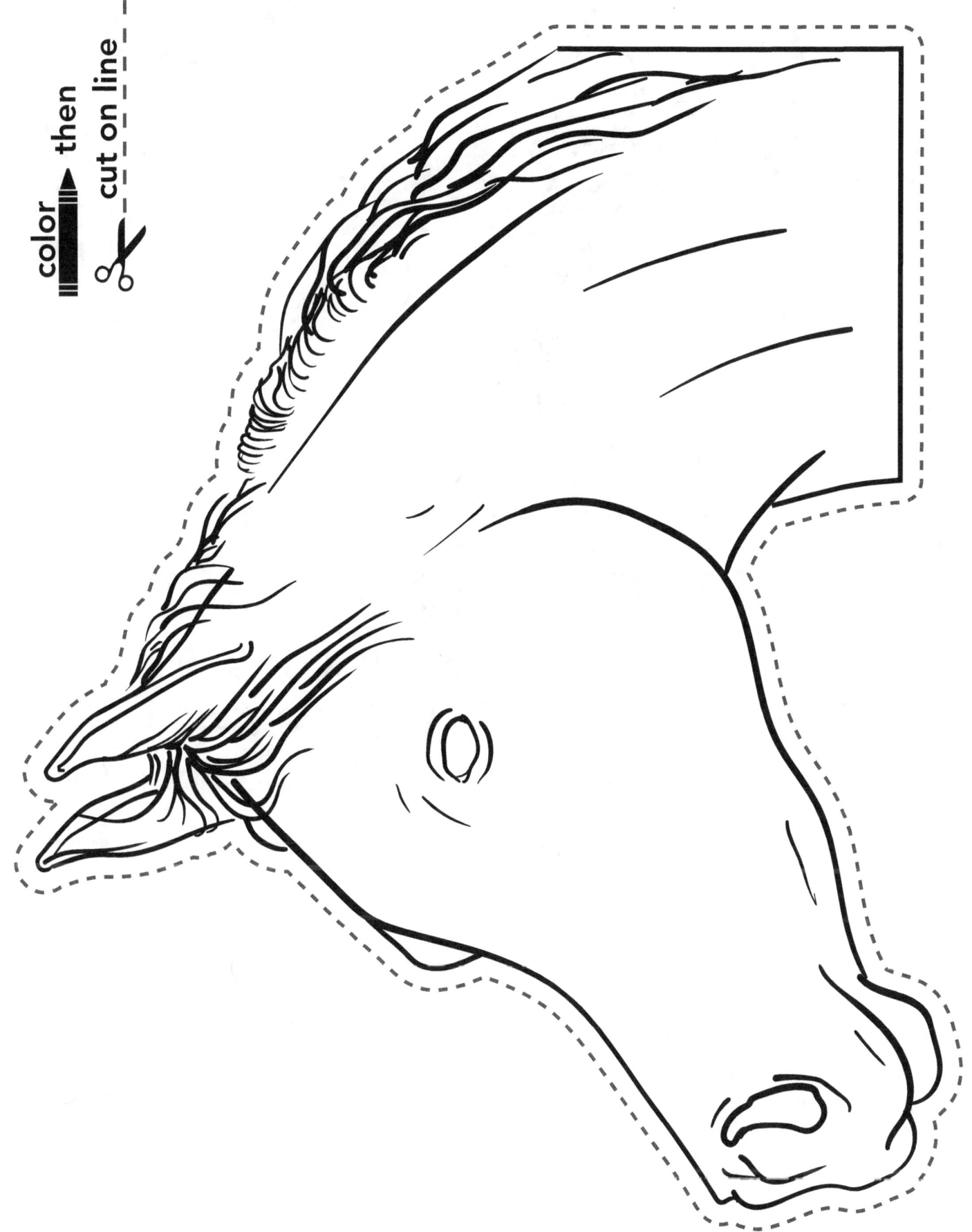

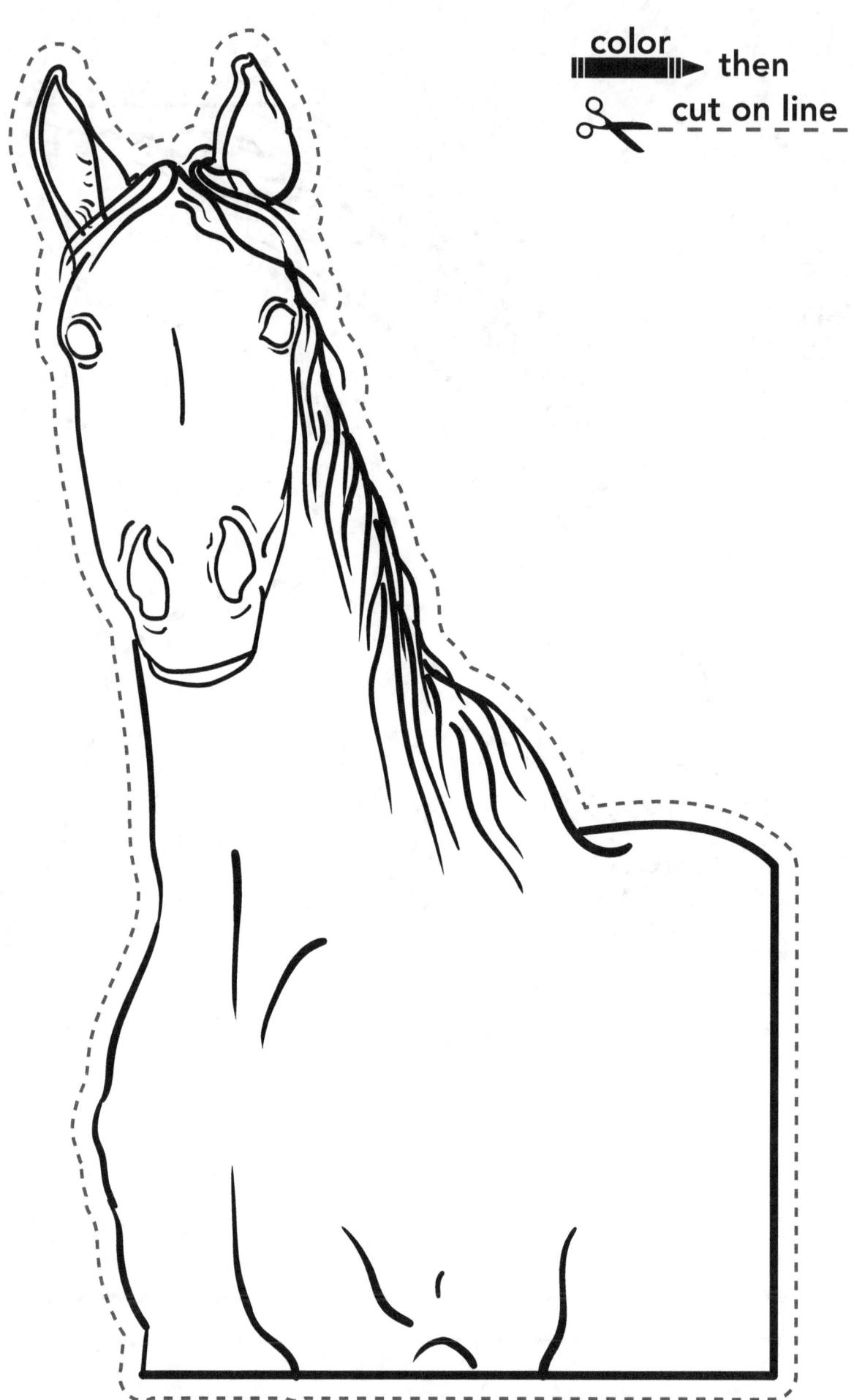

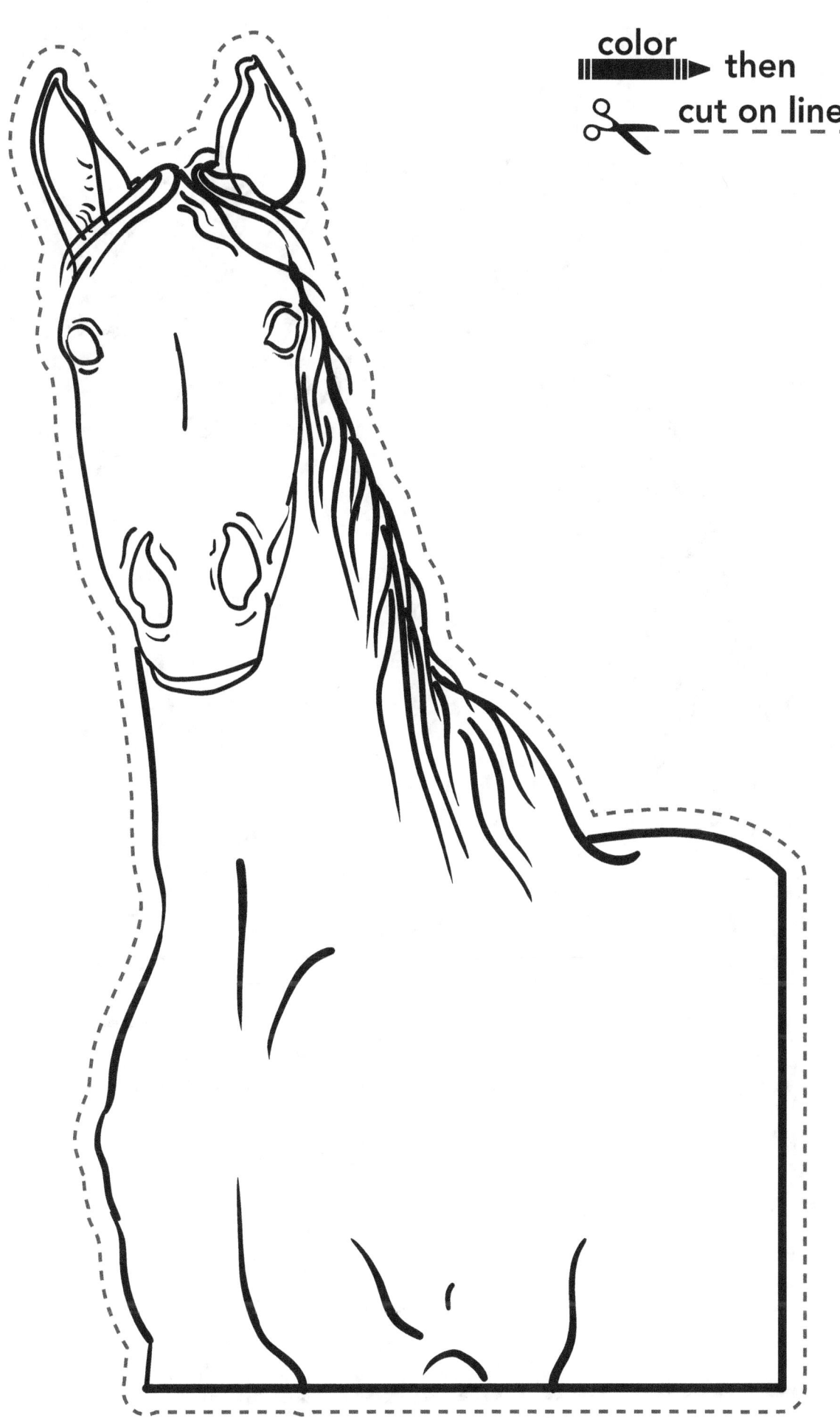

color → then
cut on line

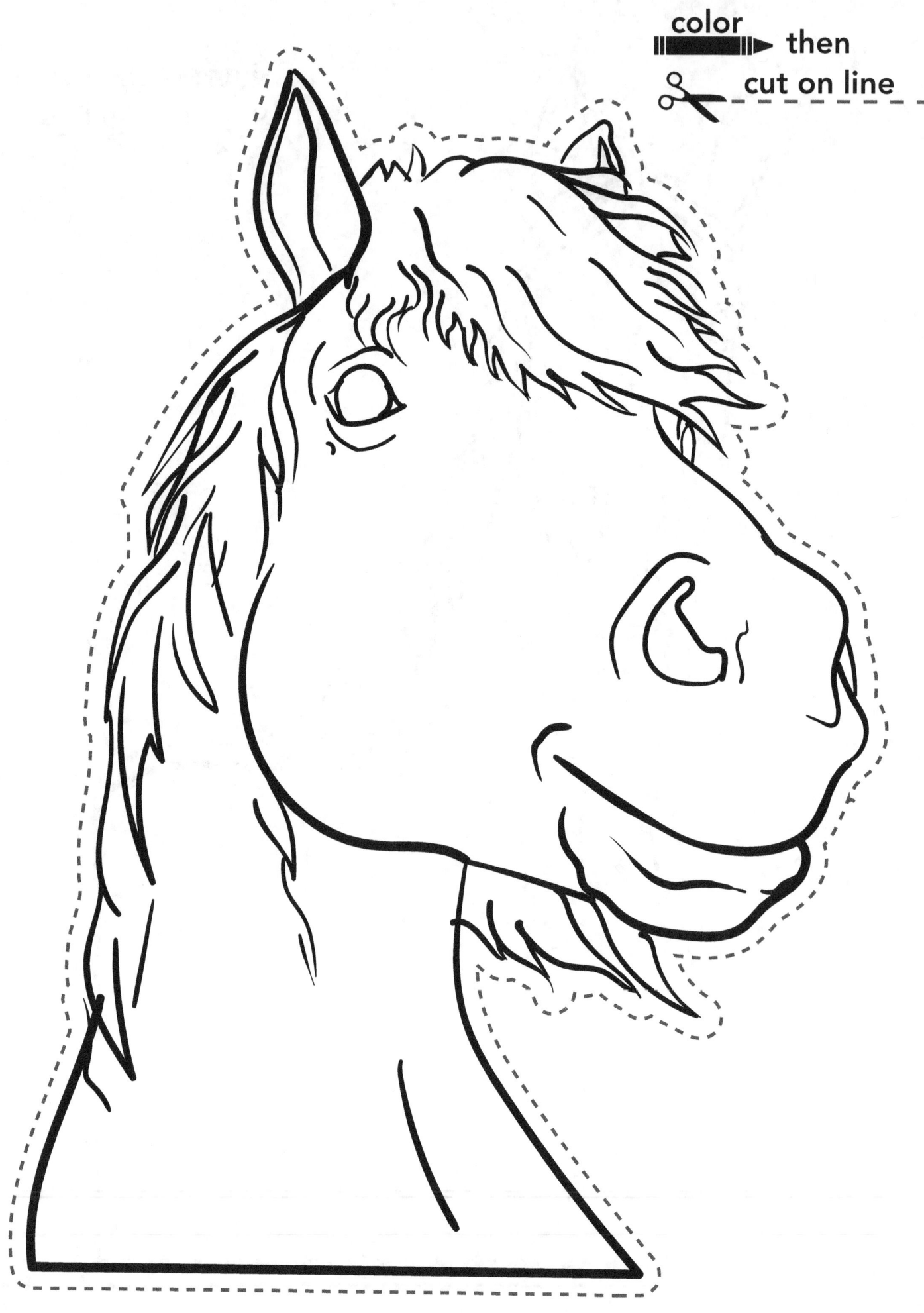

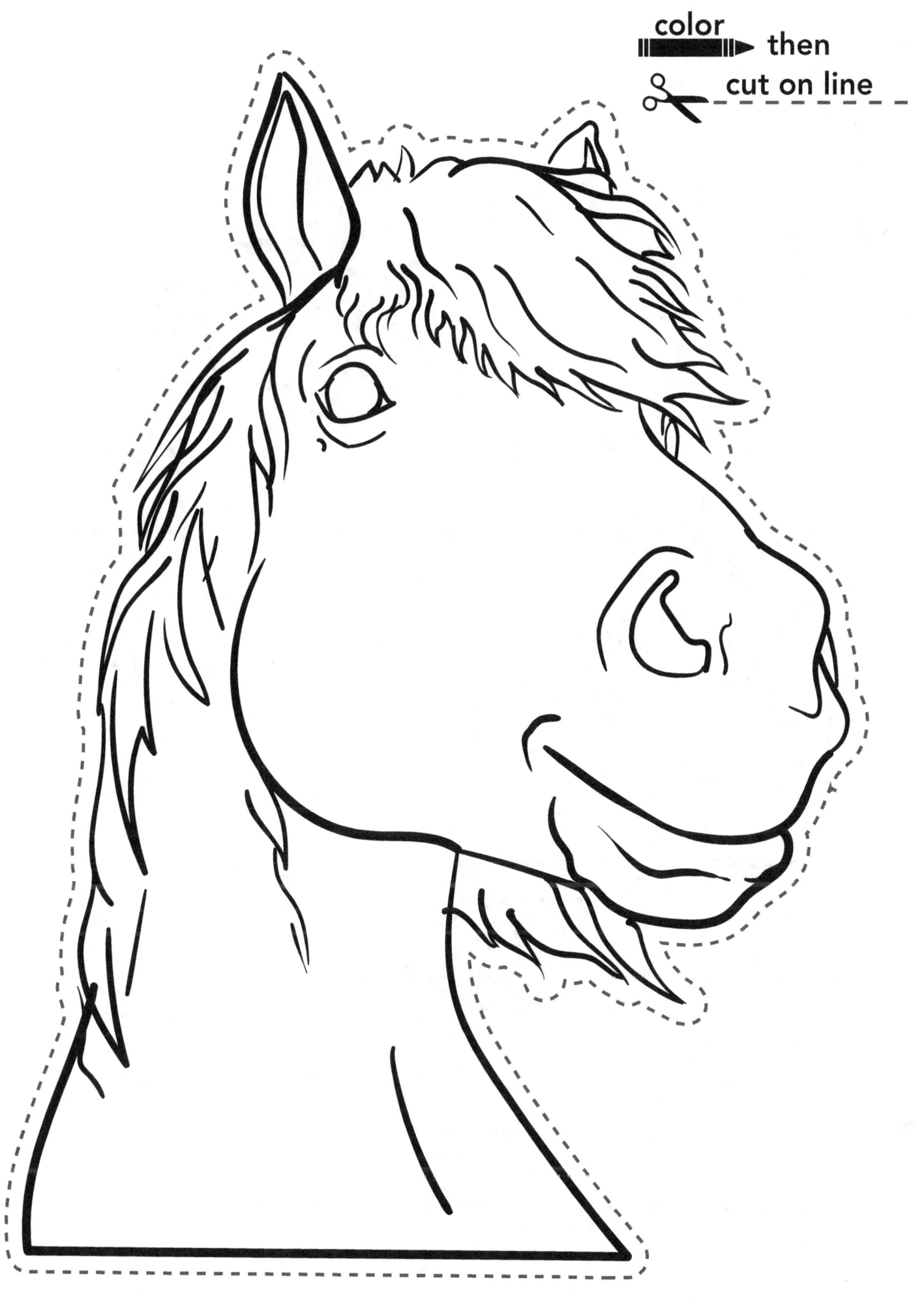

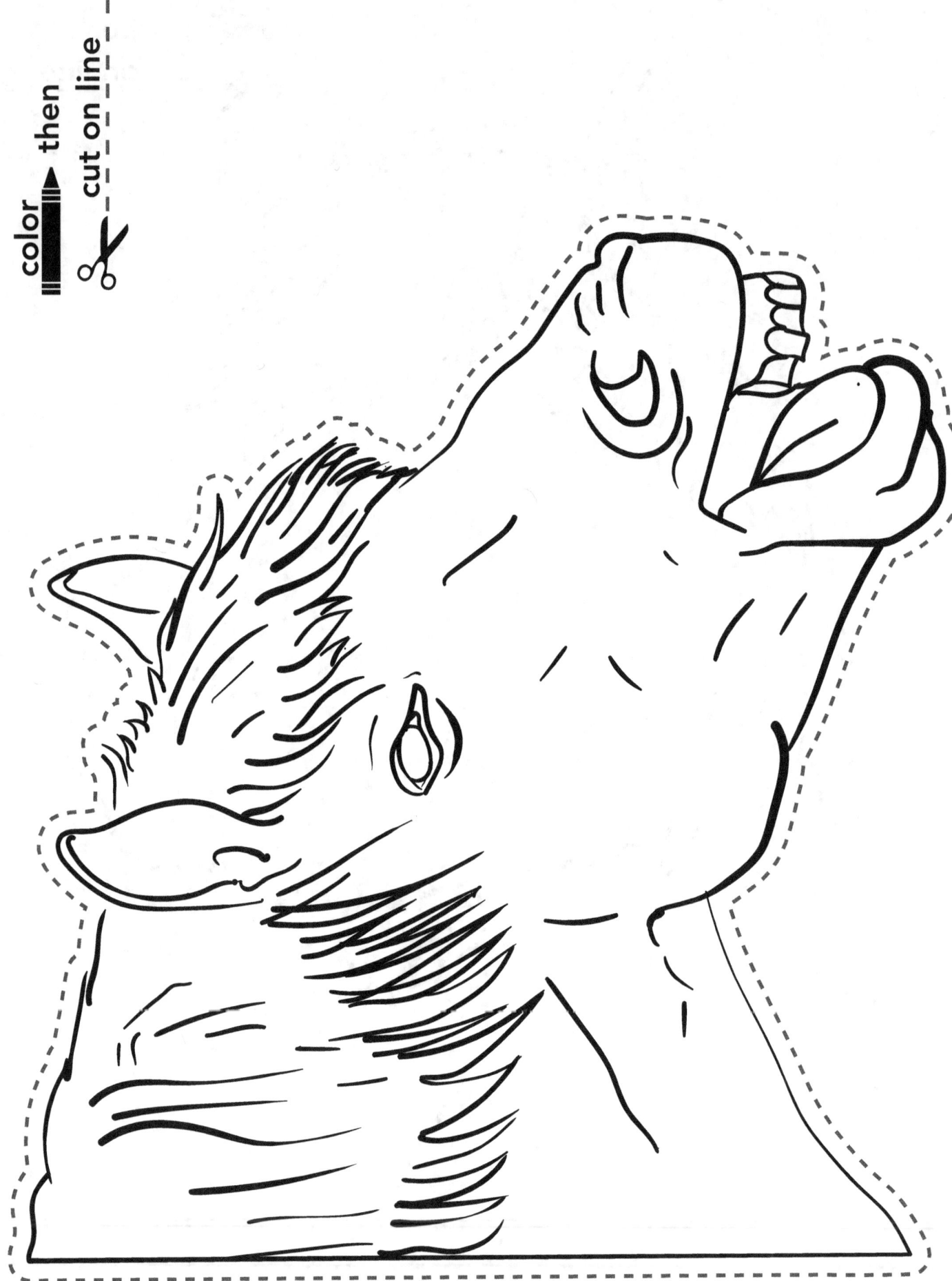

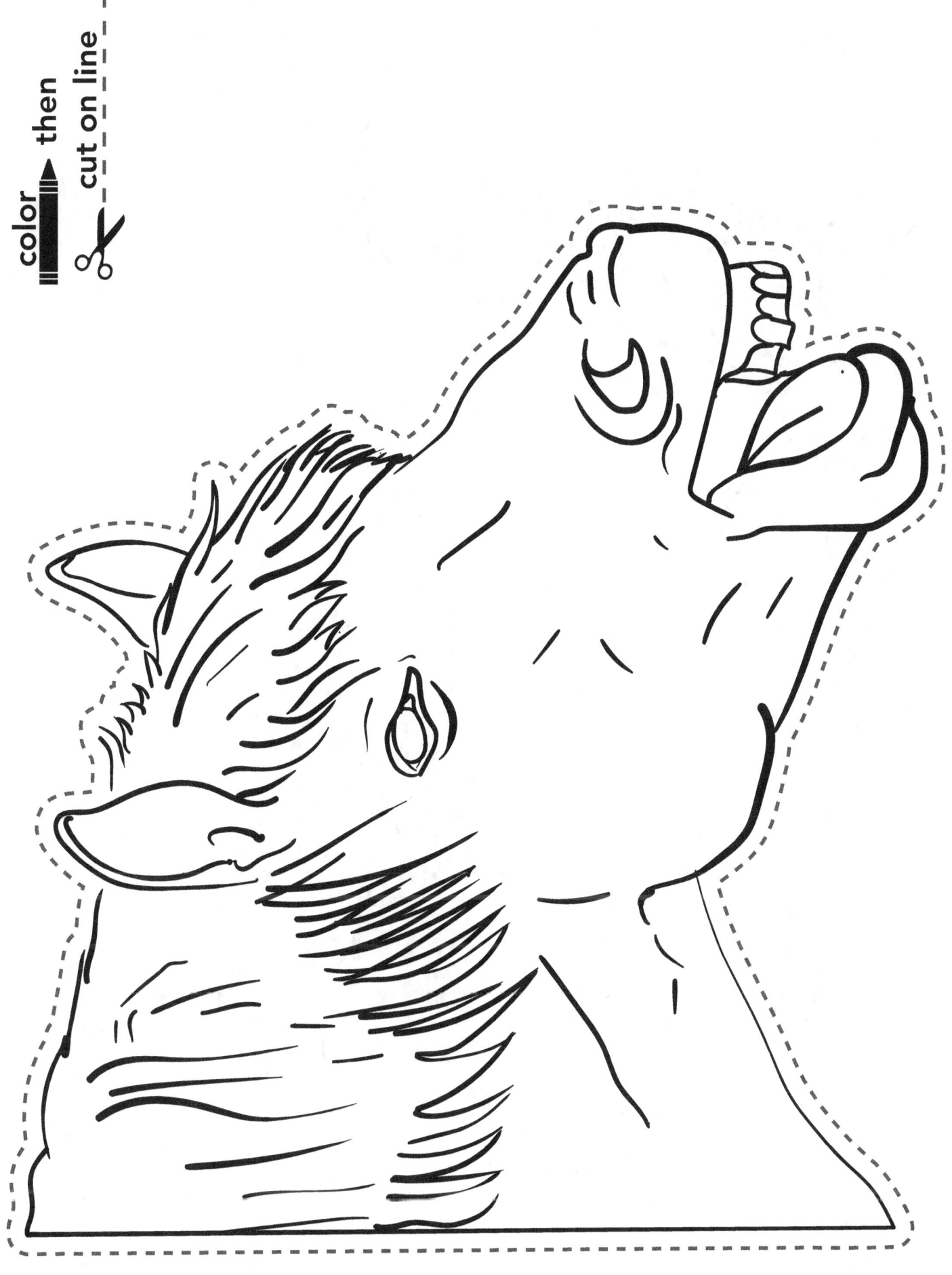

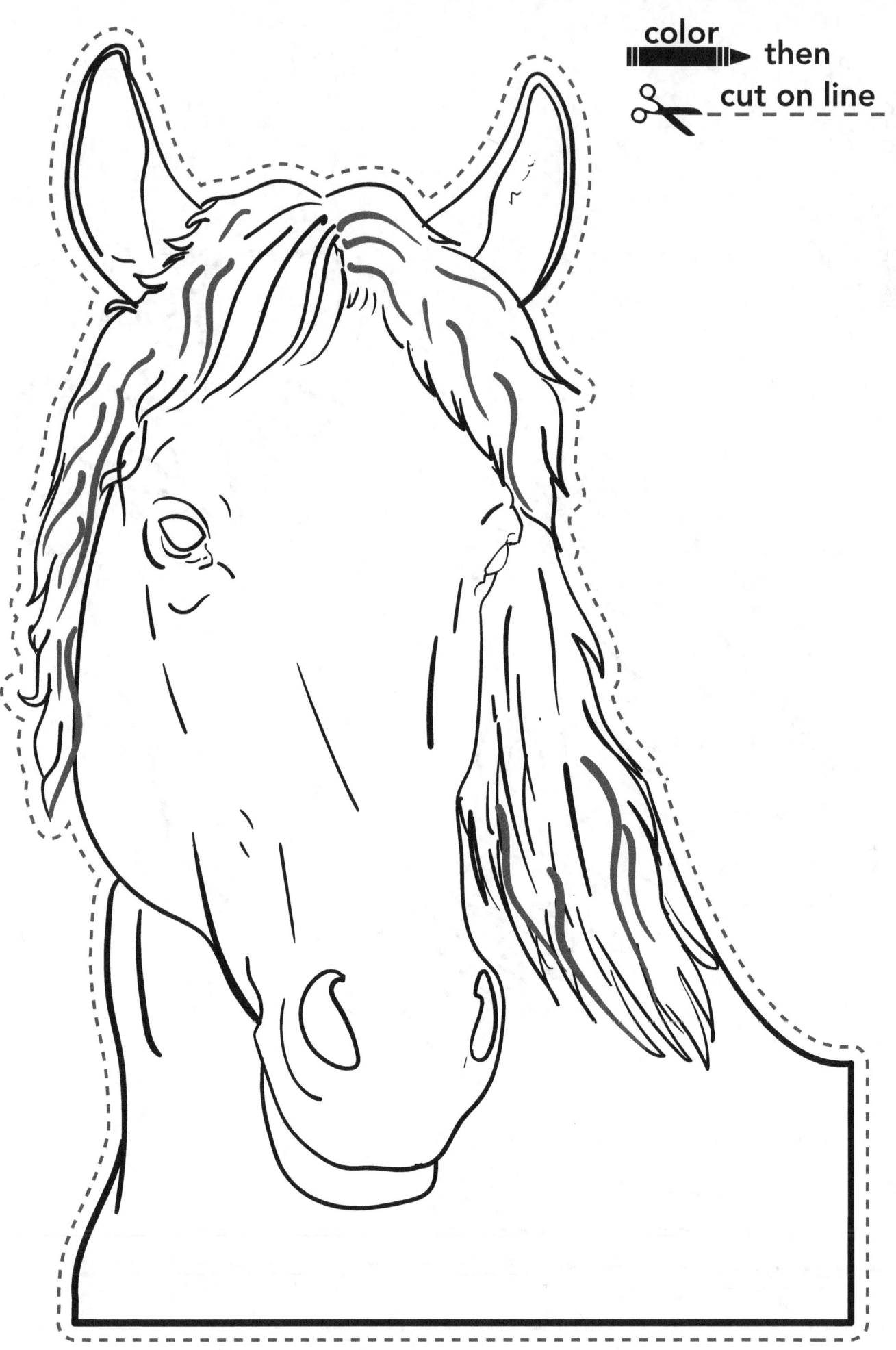

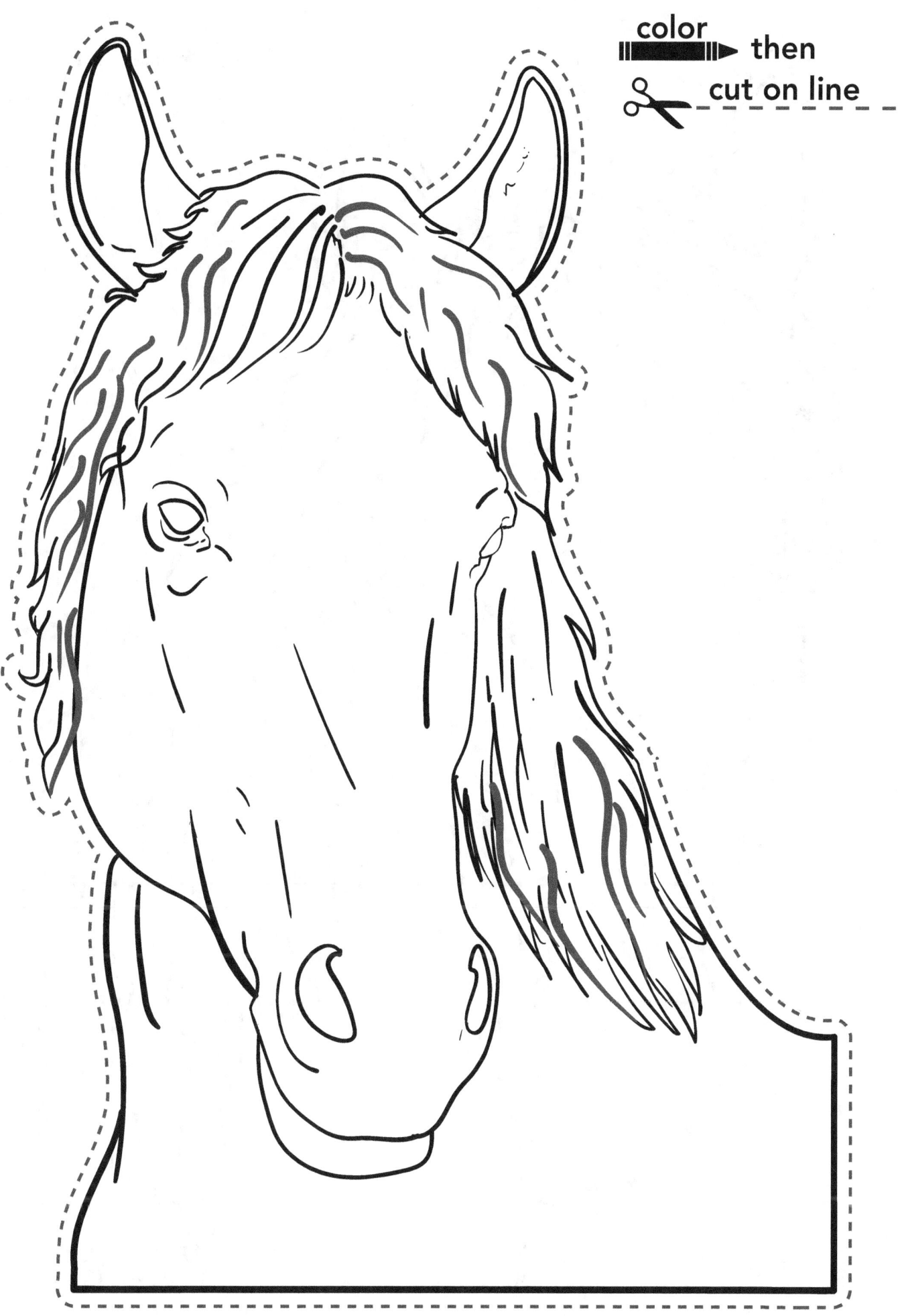

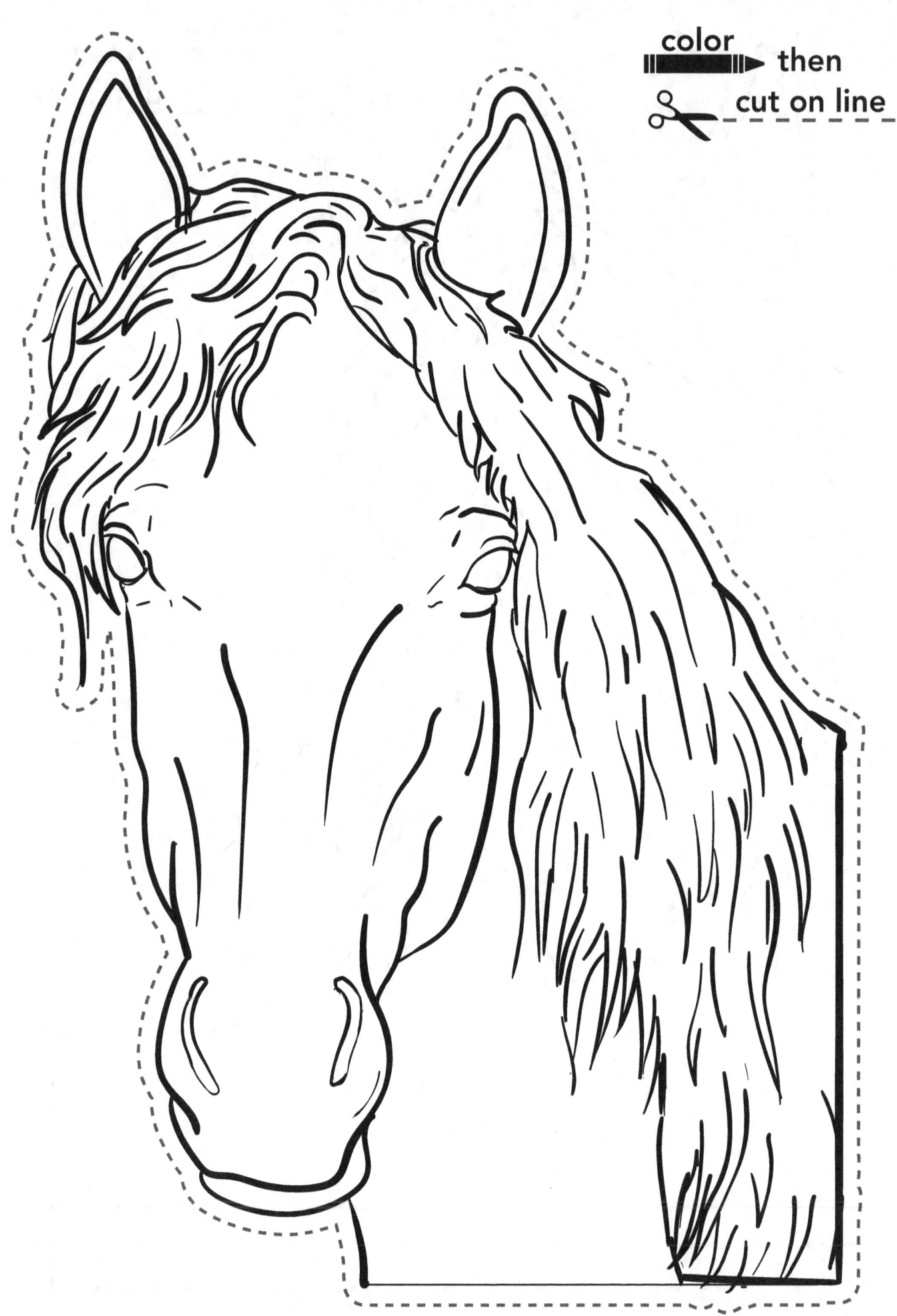

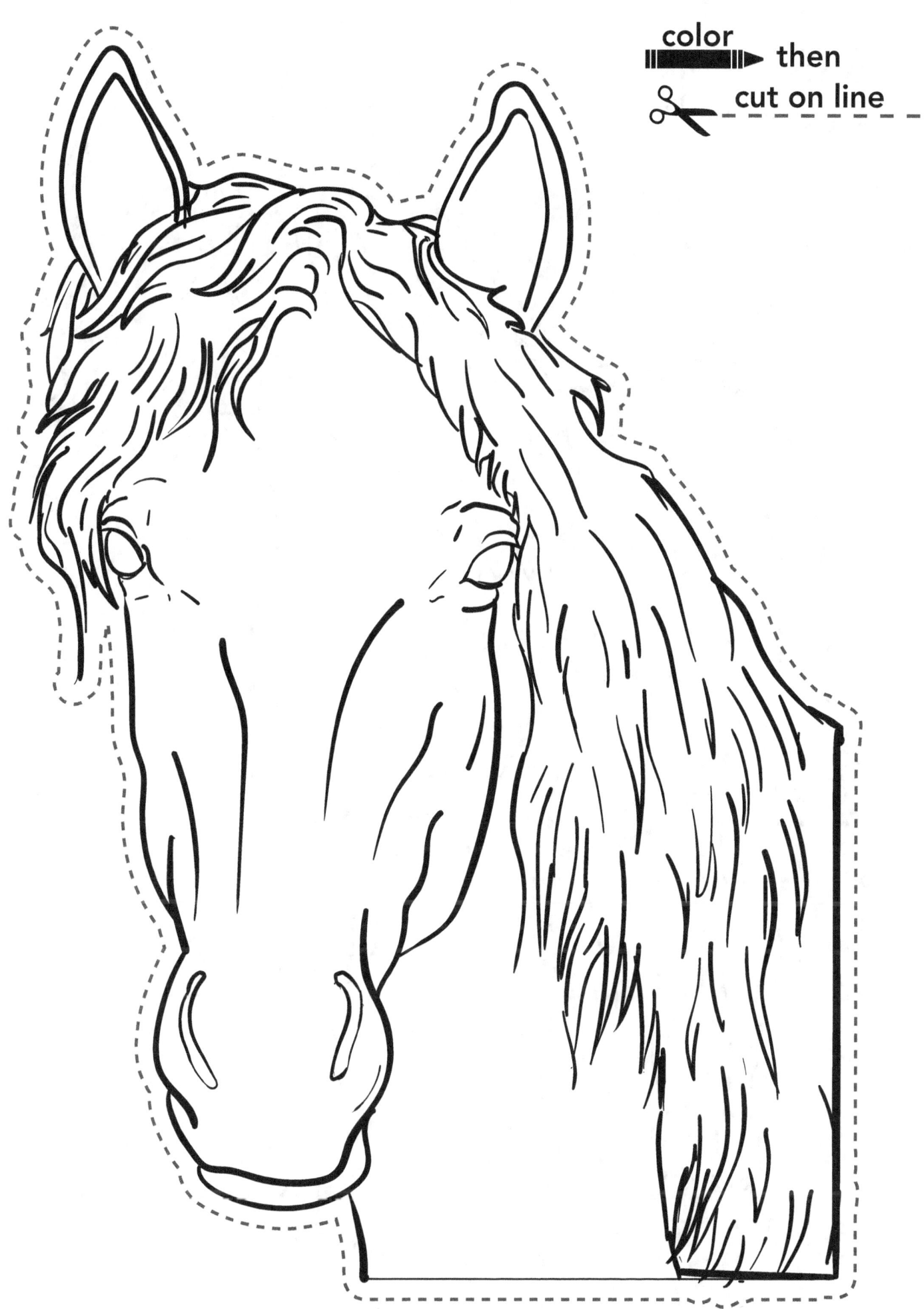

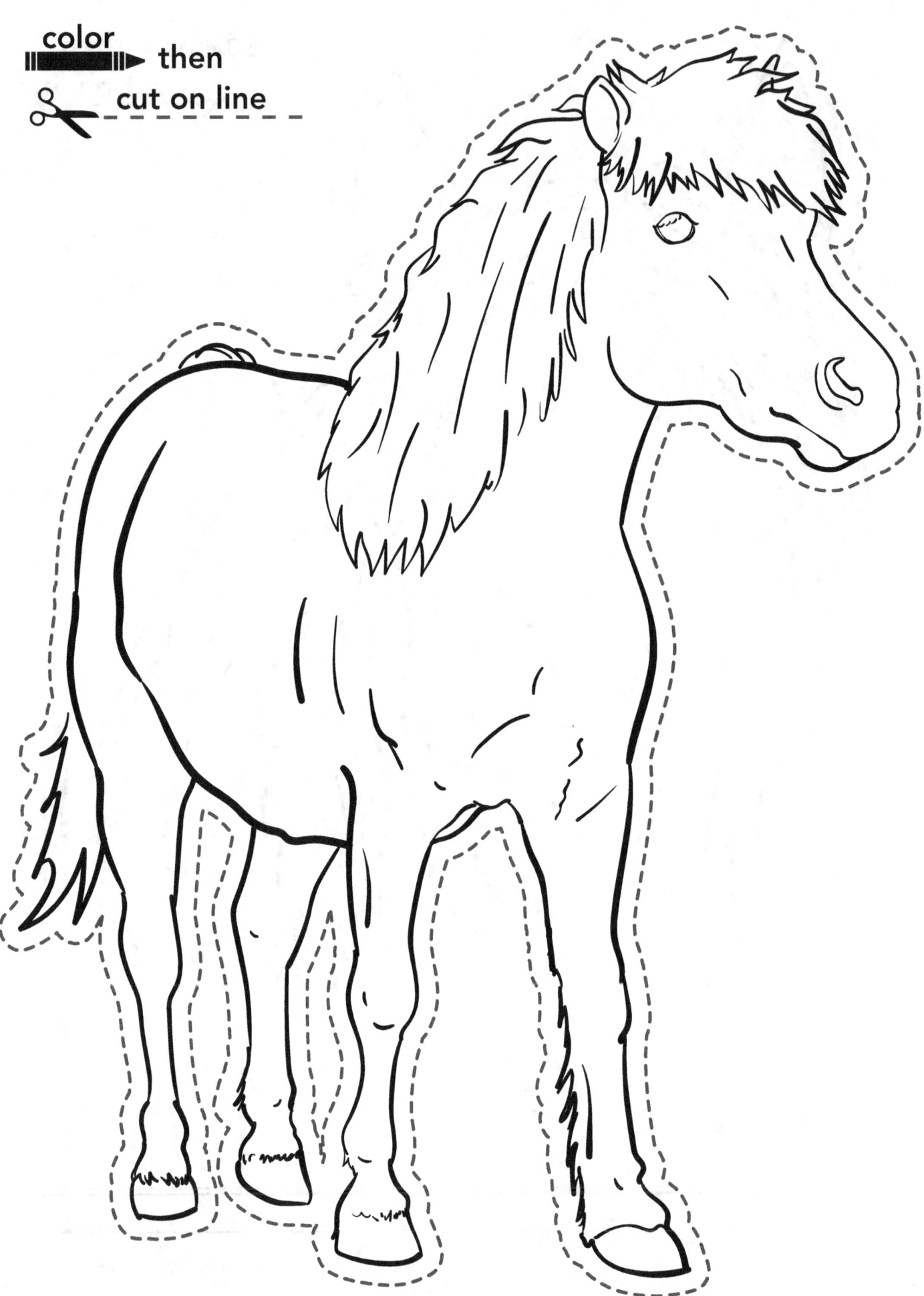

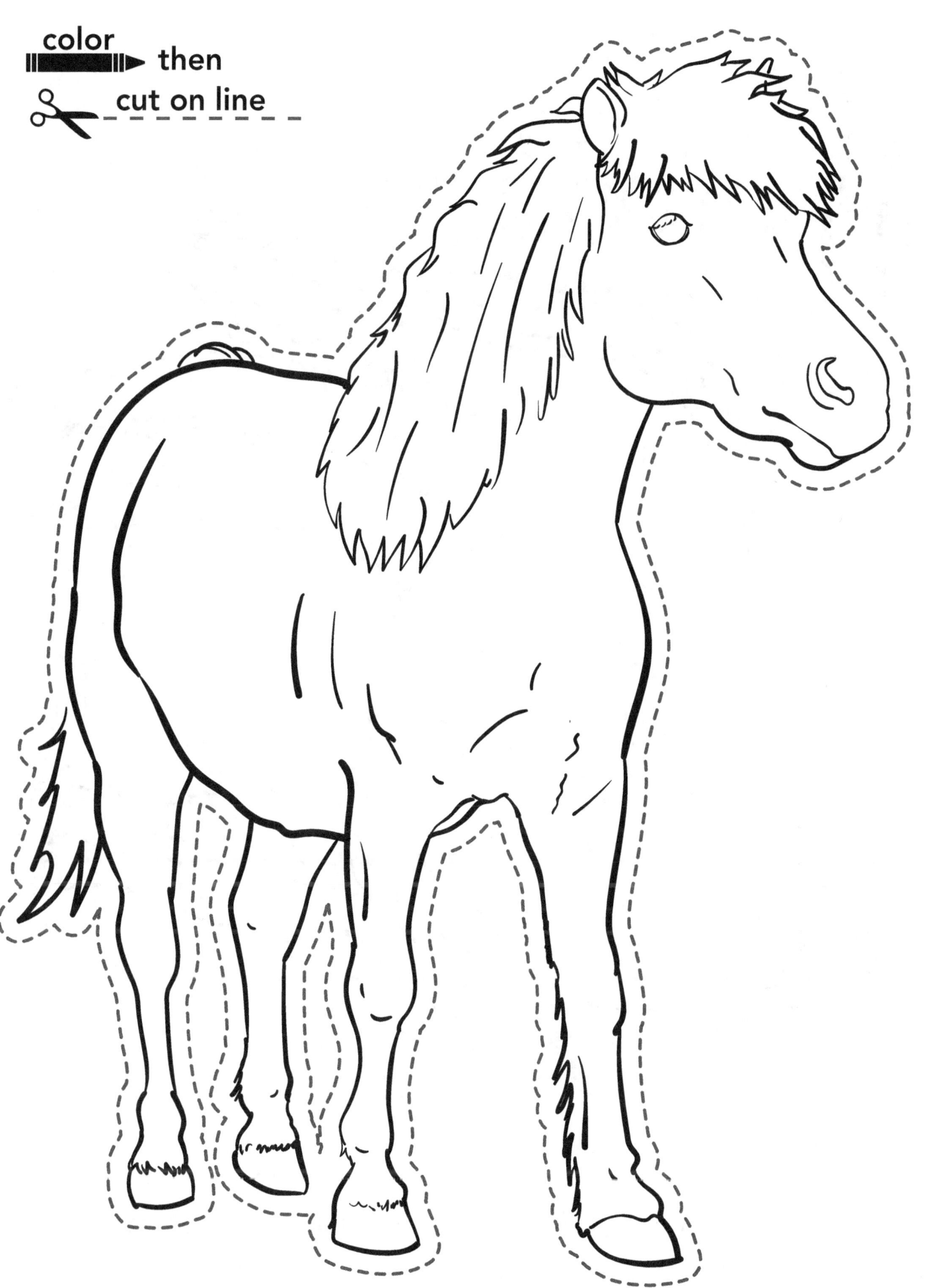

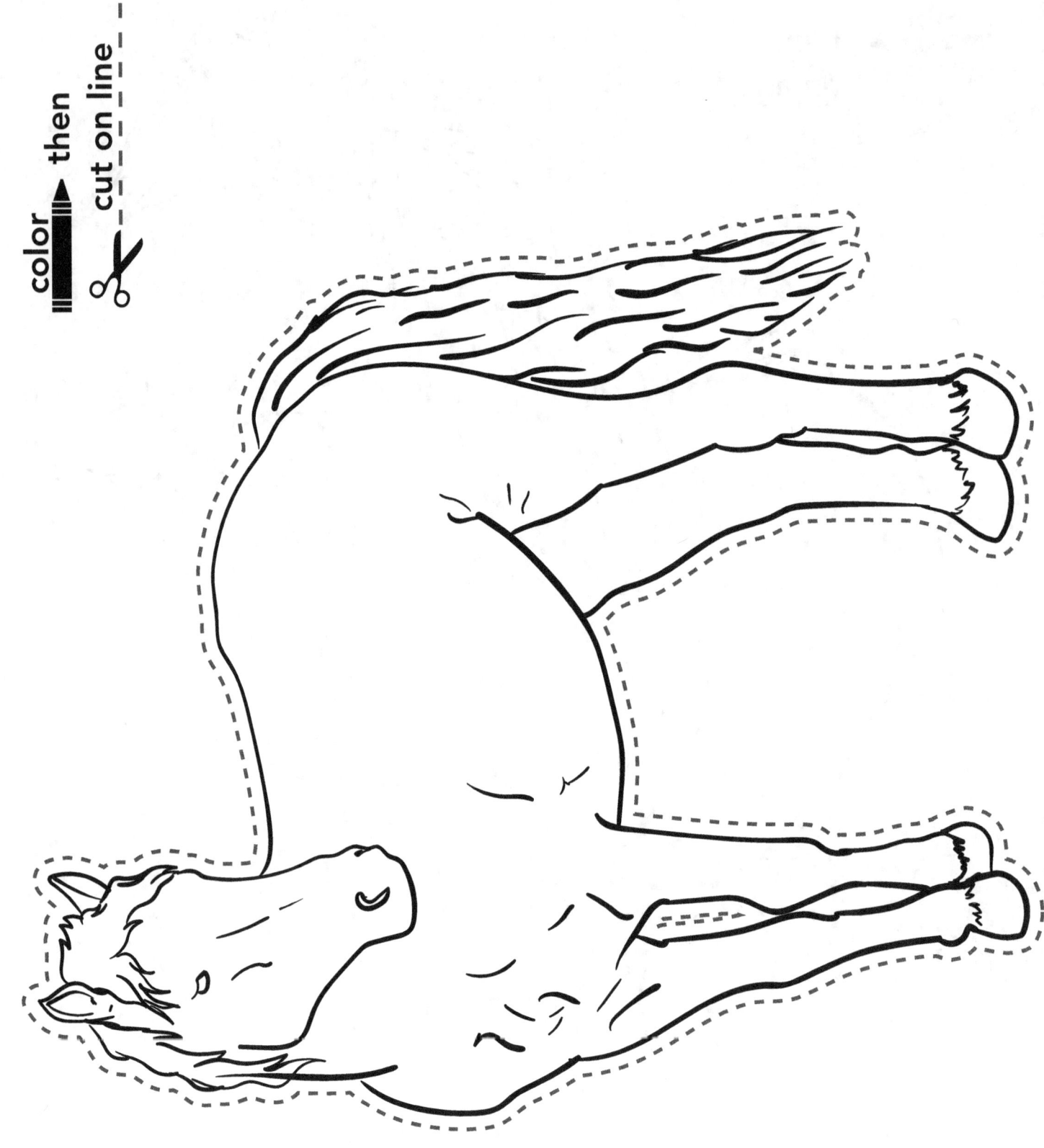

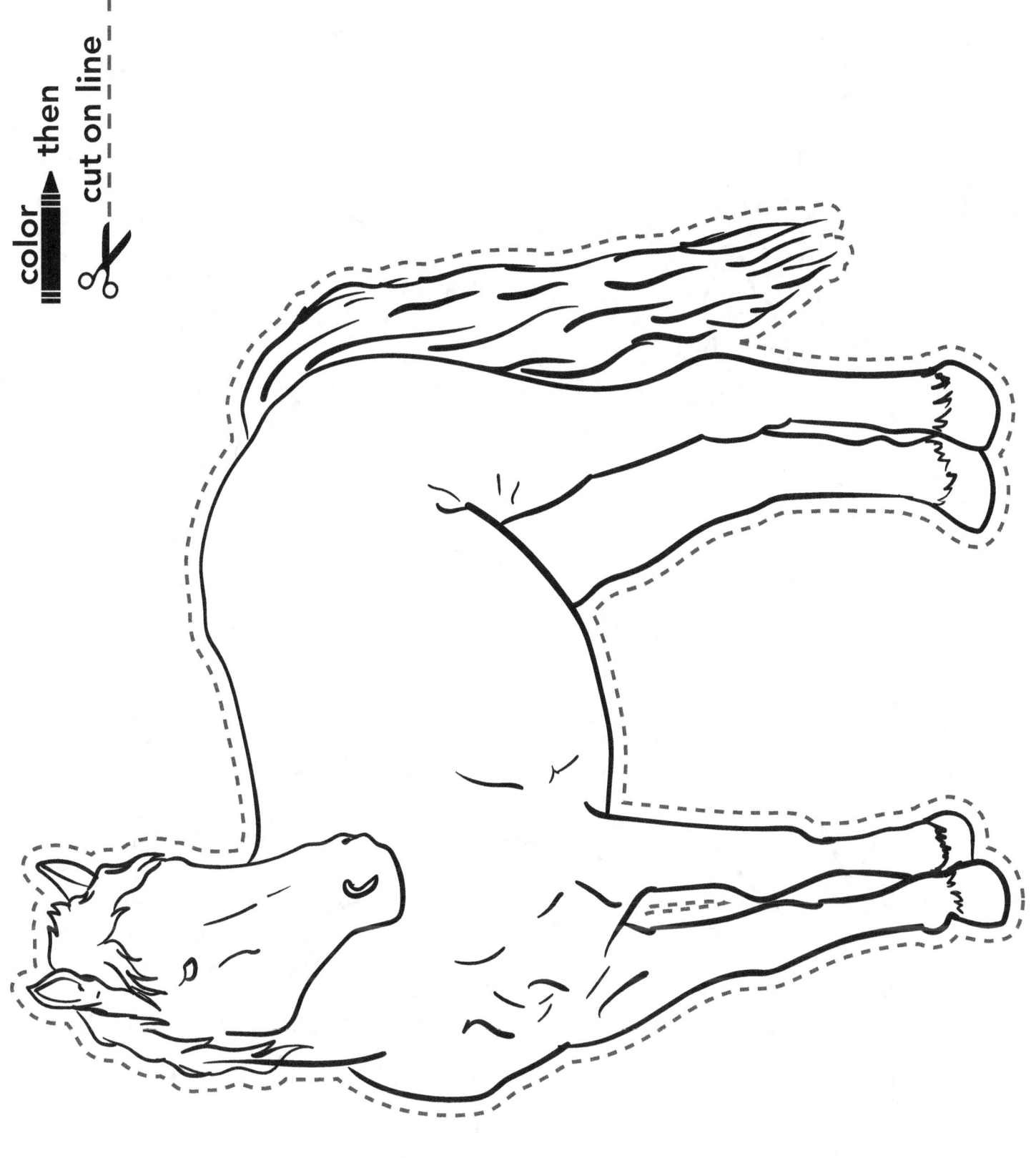

color then
cut on line

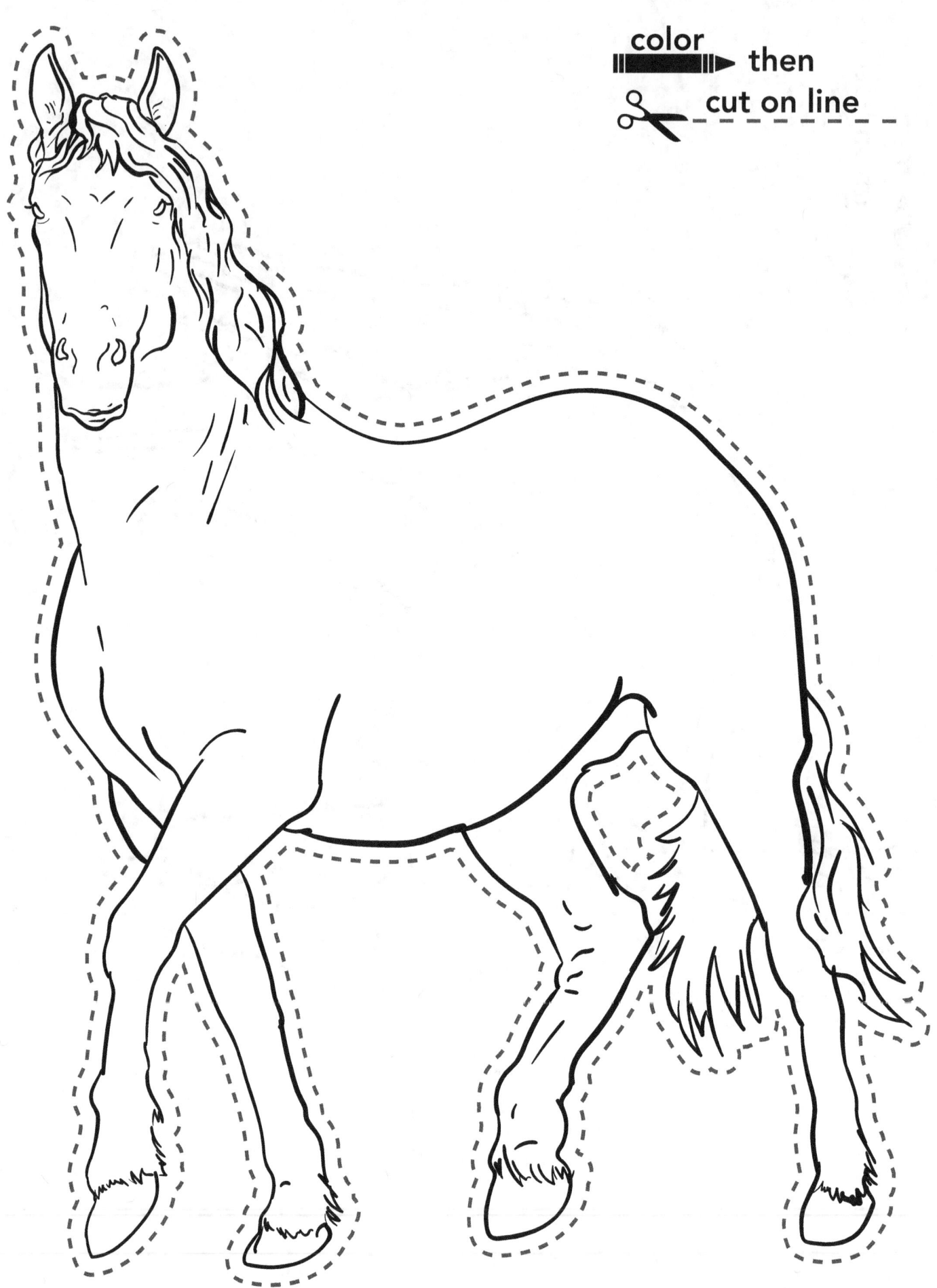

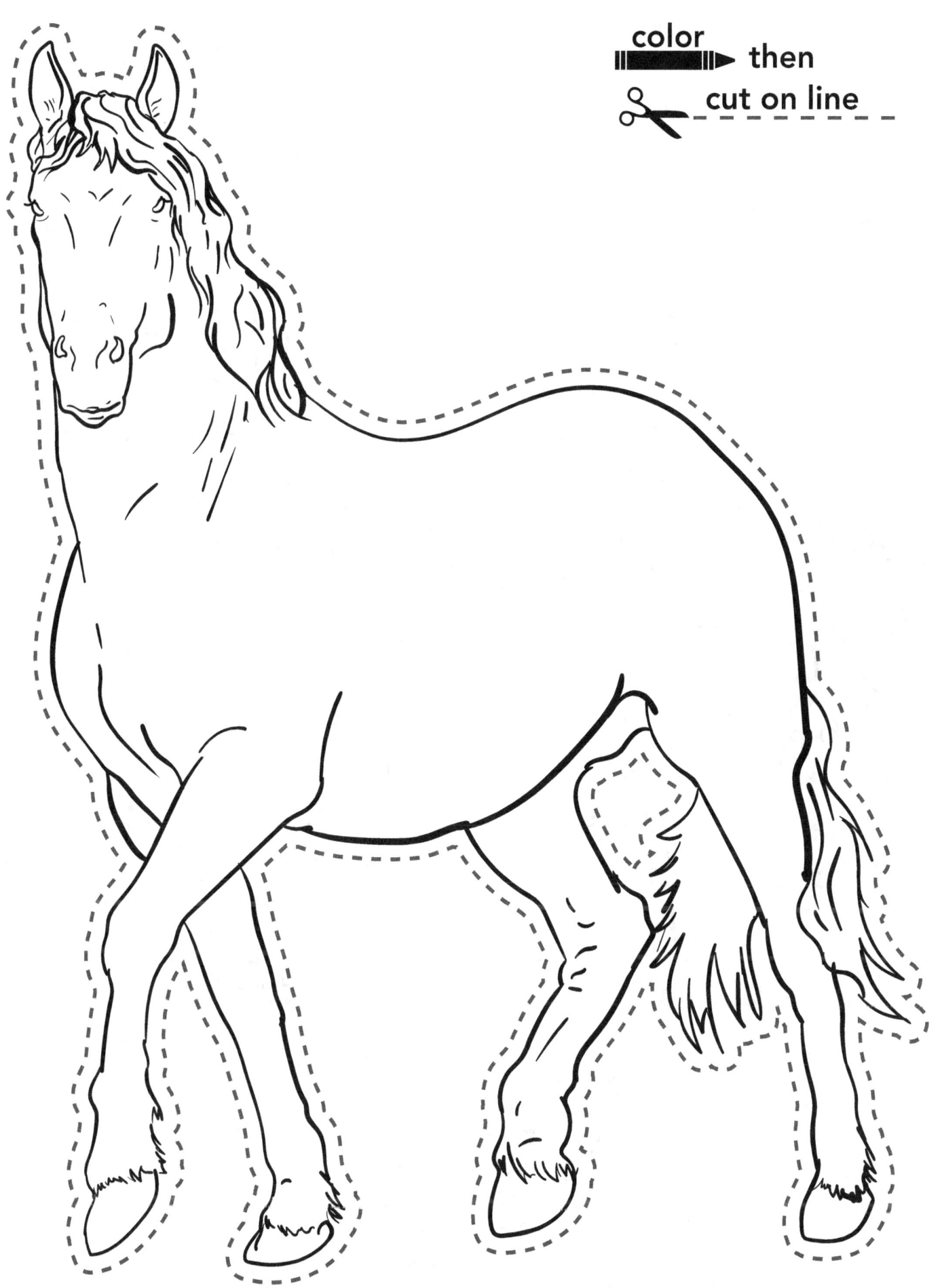

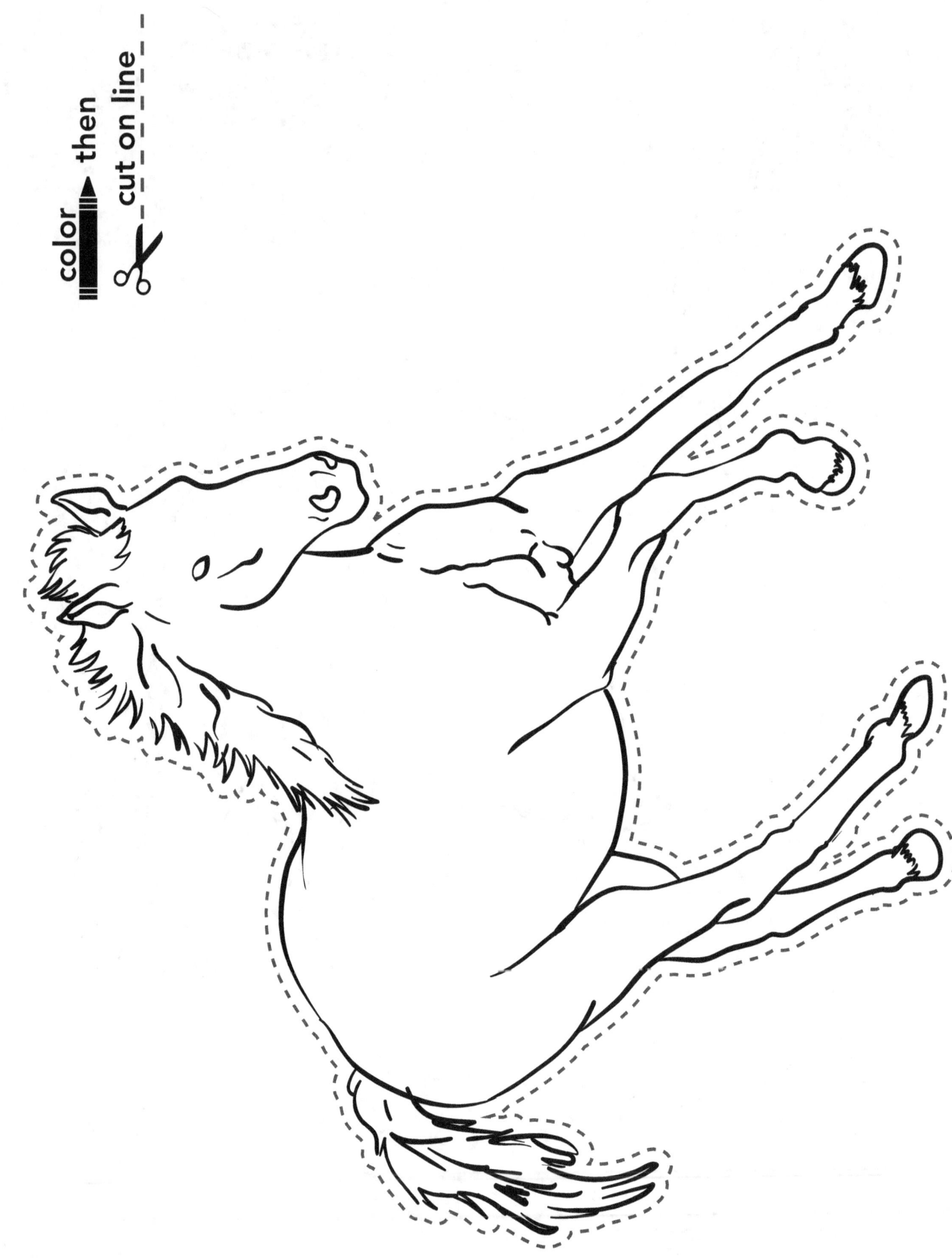

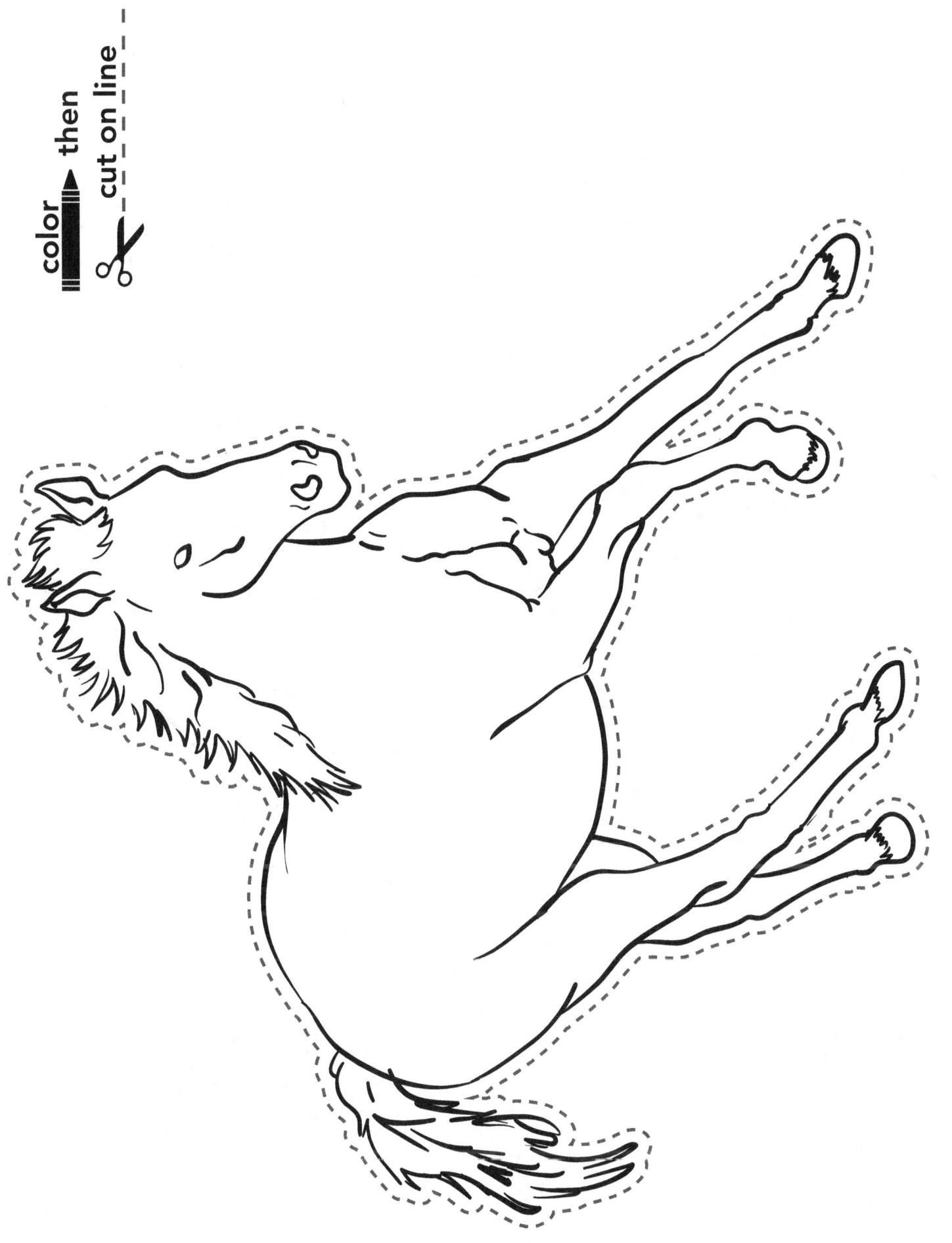

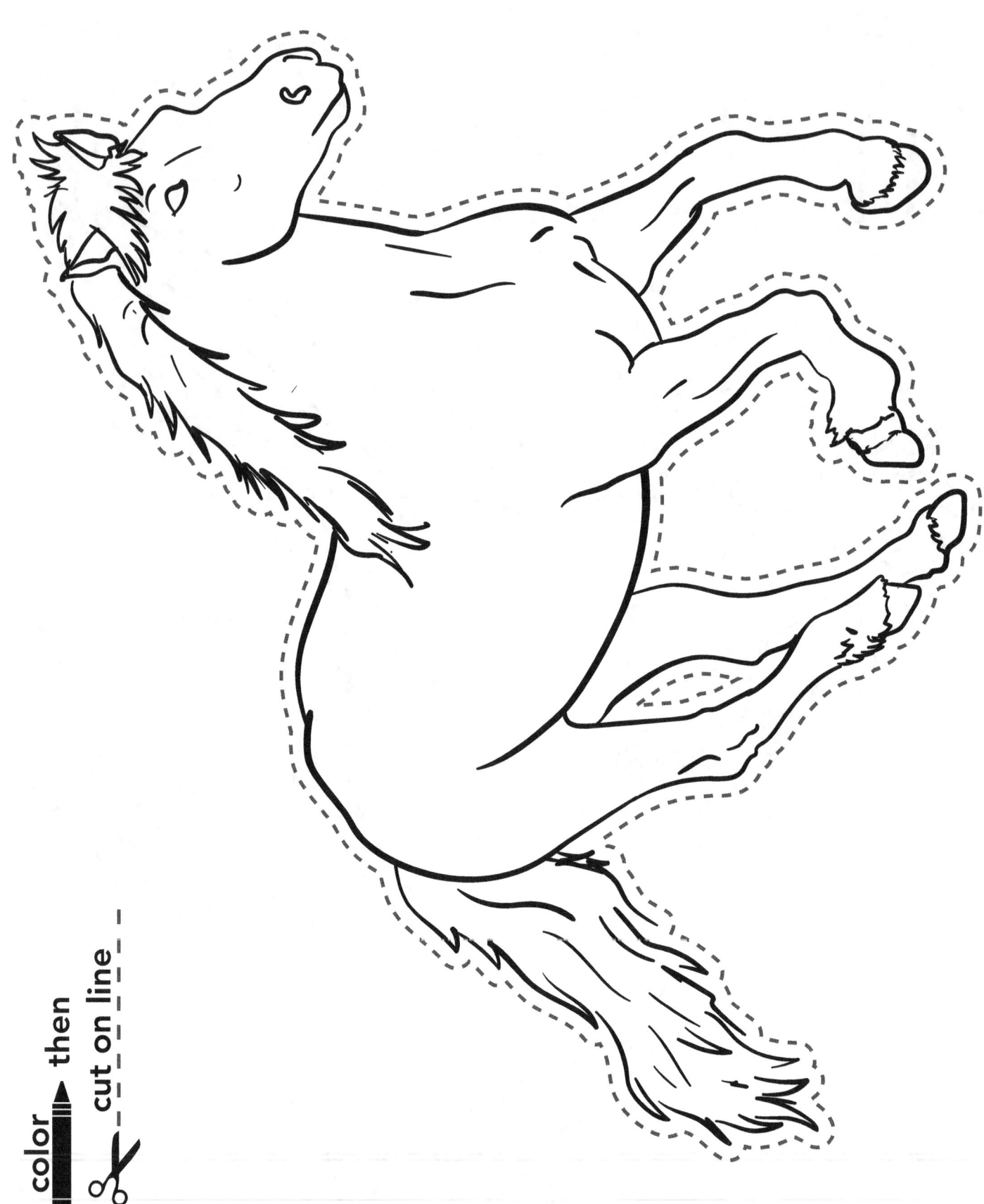

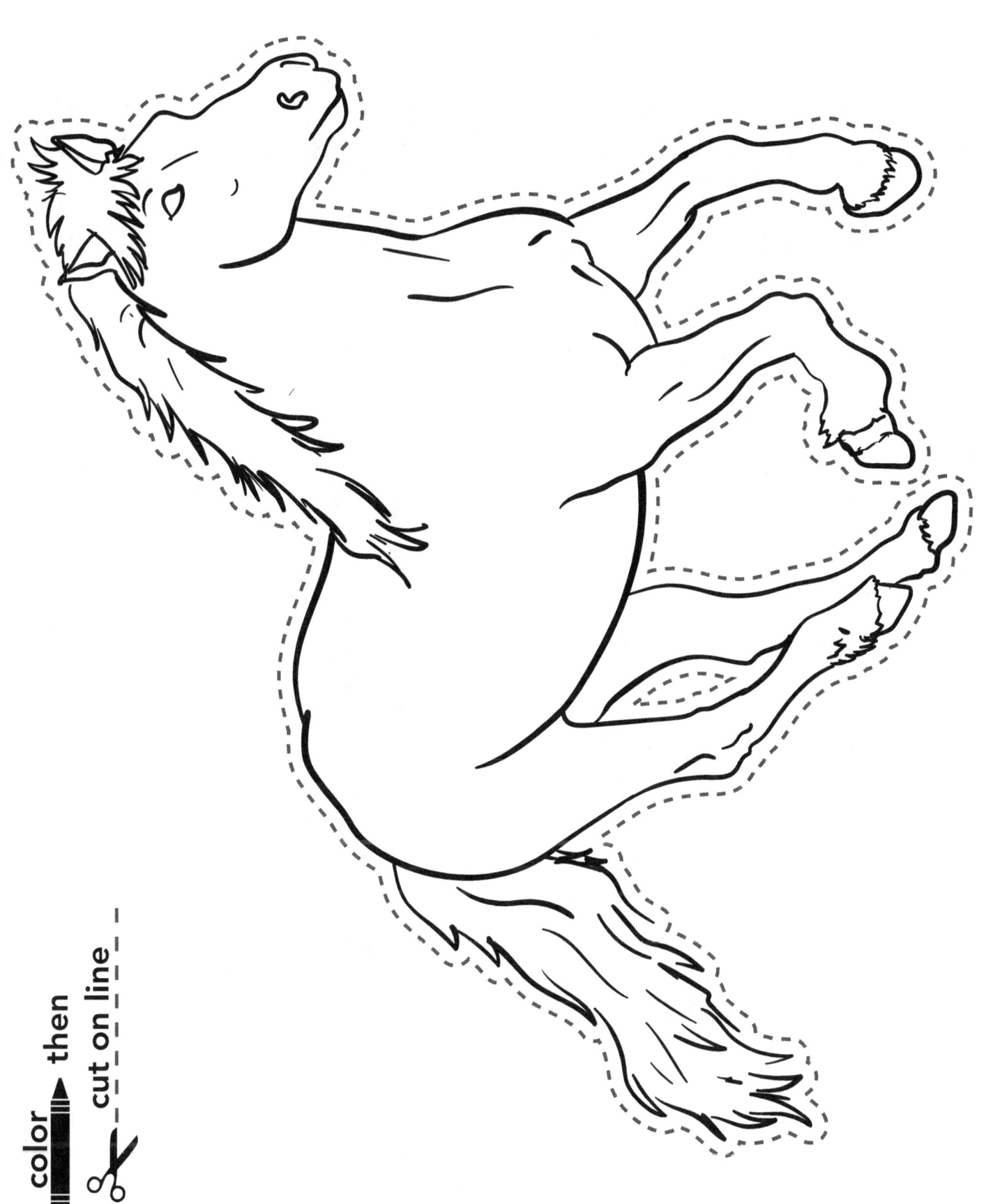

www.ingramcontent.com/pod-product-compliance
Lightning Source LLC
Chambersburg PA
CBHW080742240526
45472CB00025B/2210